I0424900

Social Change in Thailand

A. Thomas Kirsch,
a Northeastern Village, and Two Families

Edited by Yohko Tsuji
Forewords by Charles Keyes and Judy Ledgerwood

Printed by CreateSpace
Charleston, South Carolina

Front Cover Illustration:
Temple and lake in Nong Sung (photos by Yohko Tsuji) and Thai silk woven
by a Nong Sung woman (photo by William C. Ghiorse)

Copyright © 2010 Yohko Tsuji
All rights reserved.

ISBN: 1453707875
ISBN-13: 9781453707876

To the memory of Khem Tungasmita,
In-See Saendawibadhana, and Sai Saendawibadhana

A. Thomas Kirsch eating a meal in Nong Sung (1963)

Table of Contents

Preface

Eleven years have passed since my husband, A. Thomas Kirsch, Professor of Anthropology and Asian Studies at Cornell University, passed away on May 17, 1999. If he were alive, he would have celebrated his 80th birthday in 2010. To commemorate this milestone birthday and to celebrate his life, I compiled this volume. Its publication was also prompted by my wish to make past research data available for current and future scholars.

The book contains two previously unpublished articles on Thailand: "Nong Sung: A Changing Phu Thai *Tambon* (Commune) Center in Northeast Thailand" and "A Tale of Two Thai Families: Reflections on Social Change." In the first, Tom depicted life in a remote village in the early 1960s, which has virtually disappeared today. As a Harvard graduate student, he conducted his dissertation research there and wrote "Nong Sung" several years later while he was teaching at Princeton University. The second piece is my contribution. Tom's last research in Thailand in 1992 was to study the profound changes that have occurred in the Kingdom through the experiences of two Thai families—one rural and the other urban—who had "adopted" him. He had met both families during his initial fieldwork and kept in touch with them until his death. Because his cancer did not allow him to write up the outcomes of his fieldwork, the second paper is my attempt to illustrate some of these changes. Read together, I hope, these two articles disclose the tremendous changes Thai society and people have experienced over the last five decades.

This volume contains forewords by Charles Keyes and Judy Ledgerwood, two prominent anthropologists of Southeast Asia. Their forewords not only add grace to this book, but also provide a broader context in which to situate Tom's academic career and to consider the significance of his contributions. I am deeply grateful for both.

This book also has one of Tom's obituaries, "A Memoir," written by the late Oliver Wolters, his long-time colleague and friend and a renowned historian of Southeast Asia. Originally published in 2000 in the *Bulletin* of the Cornell Southeast Program, it is reprinted here by permission. I very much appreciate the Program's generosity. There are two reasons for including "A Memoir." First, it seems appropriate to add an obituary that informs readers of Tom's life. (For the same reason, I have compiled a selected list of his major works at the end.) Second, many people may not have read this obituary because the circulation of the *Bulletin* is not as large as that of Newsletter of the American Anthropological Association and *The Journal of Asian Studies* in which Tom's other obituaries appeared.

This book would not have materialized without support and encouragements of many people. In addition to those already mentioned, I would like to express my heart-felt appreciation to the two Thai families for their assistance, generosity, and friendship of nearly half a century. Both Tom and I are eternally indebted to them. Thus, it was a pleasure to have one of the grandsons of the village family as my houseguest in the summer of 2009. I hope there will be many more opportunities to reciprocate when members of both families visit America in the future.

Neither Tom nor I could have written our articles in this book without the assistance and cooperation of the villagers of Nong Sung, who originally accepted Tom into their community and always welcomed us on our subsequent visits. Moreover, on each of my two visits after his death, many of the villagers attended the Buddhist ceremony for Tom at Wat (temple) Triphun, and they prepared food and brought offerings to the service. Their warmth, generosity, and kindness deeply touched my heart. I am also grateful to the late Keawta Kanawan, a Cornell alumna, for her friendship, which lasted from my first arrival in Thailand in 1985 until her death in 2008. Keawta taught me many things about Thailand—practical, cultural, and spiritual. She made my experiences in Thailand vastly more enjoyable and much more educational and meaningful than they would have been if we had not met.

I would also like to thank Thak Chaloemtiarana who served for over a decade as the Director of the Cornell Southeast Asia Program until his retirement in 2010. Thak's wisdom and kindness helped me a great deal on various occasions. Gregory Tremblay rescued me many times when I encountered computer problems. I particularly appreciate his treatment of my computer illiteracy with patience and gentleness. Patti Butler endowed the three tables with professional looks by magically playing computer keys. Since Tom's death, Dolina Millar has been a valuable source of information about Thailand and of advice on writing in English. Audrey Kahin generously shared with me her knowledge of Southeast Asia and publication-related issues. My gratitude also goes to Gregory Green, Curator of Echols Collection on Southeast Asia, for his assistance with bibliography of Thai sources and transliteration of Thai words.

Judith Reppy and Bill Ghiorse kindly proofread the final manuscripts. Their sharp eyes caught typographical errors and other problems and saved me from some embarrassment. Bill read several earlier drafts as well. His comments and suggestions contributed to improving the clarity and style of the writing in this book. His assistance with scanning photographic images is also acknowledged with gratitude.

I owe much to the late Oliver Wolters. Not only did he write "A Memoir" with affection and respect to Tom, but also, using a historian's probe, recreated Tom's life from childhood to death, not just as a scholar, but as a person of many facets. Last, but not least, I would like to thank my late husband, A. Thomas Kirsch. He was my best friend and teacher in life, and he continues to be so in death through some mythical channel. While I, a non-Thai specialist, was writing my essay on Thailand for this volume, I was keenly aware of his presence and was guided and comforted by it. *Khop khun mak na kha* (thank you very much), Tom.

Yohko Tsuji
July 2010
Ithaca, New York

Foreword

Charles Keyes
University of Washington

In late November 1963, Jane, my wife, and I traveled from the central northeastern province of Mahasarakham to Mukdahan in what was then Nakhon Phanom province. Here we met up with Tom Kirsch, a fellow anthropologist whom we had first got to know when he had come to Cornell (where Jane and I were studying) from Harvard (where he was a student) to study Thai language. Tom, along with several others, arranged for us to travel from Mukdahan to the village of Nong Sung in Kham Cha-ii district, the village where Tom had been engaged in ethnographic fieldwork since early in 1963.

Our trip to Nong Sung had been long in the planning as both Tom and I had agreed it would be helpful for us to have some firsthand comparative impressions of the two villages in northeastern Thailand where we were carrying out our researches. Our visit to Nong Sung coincided with Tom's concluding his first fieldwork in Nong Sung and we were pleased to be able to join with him when villagers gathered to honor him at a rite known as *su khwan*, 'calling the vital essence' of a person. This rite is fundamental to the traditions of both the Phu Thai, the group with whom Tom was working, and the Lao, among whom Jane and I were making a study. This rite distinguishes both the Phu Thai and Lao from the central Thai.

Thai influences were not, however, absent from the celebration organized for Tom's leaving. In the evening a troupe of puppeteers known as *nang talung* had been hired for a performance. Although this troupe had come from central Thailand, their teachers had originally come from southern Thailand where this form of puppeteering had roots in the Malay world and was similar to the Javanese *wayang*.

Even before our meeting in Nong Sung and Tom's subsequent visit to Bang Nong Tün, the Thai-Lao village in Mahasarakham where Jane and I were carrying out our own research, Tom and I had been engaged through occasional meetings in Bangkok and more through an exchange of letters in trying to make sense of the rural worlds where we situated ourselves. We sought to understand how these worlds were shaped not only by local and ethnic traditions, but also by influences that emanated from other parts of Thailand, especially Bangkok, from neighboring countries, and from South Asia from where their Buddhist traditions ultimately originated. We also sought to decide what theoretical ideas we had encountered in graduate school and in our reading were most useful for our interpretations.

Although after graduate school we ended up at different universities – Tom first at Princeton and then at Cornell and me at the University of Washington – we continued our conversations primarily by letter but also occasionally through visits in Ithaca or Seattle and meetings at conferences. Because we shared the experience of living in villages in northeastern Thailand, we found that even when we were engaged in subsequent studies we always returned to refer to Nong Sung and Nong Tün as the foundation of our ethnographic thinking.

That our lives had been so intertwined was made poignantly apparent after Tom's death when Yohko took his ashes to be enshrined in Nong Sung. A photo from 1963 that was used in a Thai newspaper article about Tom's final return to Nong Sung misidentified Tom when, in fact, the picture was of me when I had visited Nong Sung.

I owe Tom – or Ajarn Kirsch as he was more widely known by Nong Sung villagers as well as his students and colleagues from Thailand – a great intellectual debt. He gave generously of his time in commenting on numerous papers I had written and his critiques, together with Jane's, helped me sharpen – at least to some degree – my own thinking. But most of all I owe him a deep debt of gratitude for his friendship – one that was cemented forever in that November 1963 visit to Nong Sung.

Because of the two papers that appear in this volume a wider audience can now appreciate the significance of Nong Sung for Tom. The first paper is one that has been recovered from an aborted project by another colleague who had planned to bring together a number of short ethnographies of villages in Thailand. (My own paper on Nong Tün for that volume still remains unpublished.) Tom wrote this paper only a relatively short time after he had completed his research in Nong Sung. It is, thus, close to the ethnographic time that it refers to even though it is appearing decades later. As I have become aware in my own engagement with my field notes and earlier writings, the anthropologist needs to be aware that one's work becomes historical records as much as it consists of ethnographic accounts.

Yohko's paper accentuates the historical character of the anthropologist's engagement with the places in which he lives and carries out fieldwork. Yohko shows how the linkages between Nong Sung and Bangkok that in 1963 were primarily evident in Tom's own movement between these places increasingly came to blur the distinction between the urban and the rural. This blurring has, however, become a source of conflict in contemporary Thailand now that the demands of 'rural' people – who often live and work in Bangkok – for a larger voice in the Thai political system are resented by the old and even new established upper and middle classes in Bangkok. This is, however, another story. Through the papers that have been brought together in this volume, one can gain insights into a rural world that has essentially disappeared and into the lives of the people who have through their choices brought the rural and urban of Thailand closer together. And most of all these papers are a tribute to Tom Kirsch, a great scholar and ethnographer and a loving husband and great friend.

Foreword

Judy Ledgerwood
Northern Illinois University

A. Thomas Kirsch was my teacher in the Anthropology Department at Cornell University; I am indebted to him for many reasons. He was one of the key people, along with David Wyatt and O.W. Wolters, who created the paradigmatic models on Southeast Asia and made them come alive for me in the classroom: "men of prowess," prestige systems, kinship systems, trading networks and Buddhist practice. I knew Southeast Asia through the lectures and writings of these men and other early scholars like Lucian and Jane Hanks, Ben Anderson and Charles Keyes. This is the scaffolding upon which I and other scholars of my generation stood as we went off and conducted research and published our own work.

Returning to Nong Sung in 1963 with Tom Kirsch in this mini-ethnography reminds us of the painstakingly detailed ethnographic work that went into gathering and analyzing the data that were the seeds of those paradigms. Who were village leaders? How did they earn the respect of their fellow villagers 50 years ago? And even then how was "national" Thai culture changing village religious beliefs and social relations? Dr. Kirsch's comments on teachers as conduits for this "Thaicizing" process are all the more fascinating given the lives of the schoolmaster's children and grandchildren.

But Dr. Kirsch was never locked into or limited by a particular paradigm or model. This report from 1963 tells us of a statistical dominance of virilocal residence and a virilateral bias in the inheritance of rice land and parental houses – in contrast to reported preferences for uxorilocal residence and inheritance of the parent's house by youngest daughters across northeastern Thailand. The writing "hovers" close to the ethnographic details, never far from the stories of people emplaced in a particular moment.

I am keenly aware now as I head off to the field in Cambodia, to conduct field work where my other mentor May Ebihara conducted her field work in 1959-60 and later in the 1990s, of the responsibility I have to continue this style of ethnographic work. Tom Kirsch's work in Nong Song and May Ebihara's in Sabaay are the foundations upon which the Anthropology of Southeast Asia have been written. I hope to track down the children and grandchildren of those Dr. Ebihara interviewed 50 years ago, as Yohko Kirsch Tsuji has done, and track a parallel trajectory from rural to urban spaces and from isolation to integration into very complex global networks.

Having this document in print is one final lesson from the teacher Dr. Kirsch, and his wife, on Thai society, anthropology, research methods and the dynamism of social change.

Nong Sung

A Changing Phu Thai *Tambon* (Commune)[1]
Center in Northeast Thailand

A. Thomas Kirsch

Introduction

Despite underlying similarities of language and culture, Northeast Thailand has historically been characterized by a considerable degree of ethnic complexity. This ethnic complexity is marked even today by dialect differences, local variations in custom, and specialized ecological adaptations. The Phu Thai are one of a number of ethnic enclaves which have made the Northeast into a complex mosaic of cultural differences.

According to their own traditions, the Phu Thai migrated some 125-150 years ago to Northeast Thailand from a locality in Laos south of the modern Lao town of Savanakhet. Today there are four main concentrations of Phu Thai in the Northeast. One Phu Thai center is in the vicinity of the Lake Nong Hang in Sakhon Nakhon province. Another is in the Kuchinarai district of Kalasin province. The remaining clusters of Phu Thai are both located in Nakhon Phanom province, one centering on the village of Renu Nakhon, near the town of That Phanom, the other in Khamchai district, roughly thirty miles due west of the Mekong river town of Mukdahan. There are also some Phu Thai settlements remaining in Laos and a cluster of Phu Thai—locally known as Lao Song—living in the Central region of Thailand near Phetburi. The village of Nong Sung in which I worked in 1962-63 is located in the Khamchai district (see Map One). [2]

---

[1] Though the word, "commune," may have several connotations in English, in this article the term is used strictly to designate the administrative unit, "*tambon*," according to the convention of Thai studies (footnote added by Yohko Tsuji).

[2] Fieldwork on which this report is based was carried out between July, 1962 and January, 1964. My research was supported by National Institutes of Mental Health pre-doctoral Fellowship MH-12, 050 and research grant supplement M-2448. I gratefully acknowledge this assistance.

MAP ONE: Outline Map of Thailand Showing Phu Thai Localities and Important Cities.

Contemporary Phu Thai still maintain a degree of ethnic separation from both nearby Thai-Lao neighbors and from the Thai of the Central region. Despite this continued ethnic separation, Nong Sung villagers have changed and are changing: becoming more "Thai-icized" and more "Buddha-ized." Such changes have been encouraged by the efforts of the Central government to incorporate the peoples of the Northeast into a national administrative structure, to integrate them into a national political and economic system, and to assimilate them to a national Thai culture that is spread by the national schools and is based largely on the practices of the Bangkok-dominated Central region. At best, the success of the Central regime's efforts has been uneven throughout the Northeast. Many of the changes which have occurred in Nong Sung social life appear to be in directions encouraged by the government. Some of the more dramatic changes manifested in contemporary village life, e.g. those in the religious sphere, seem to owe as much to local initiatives and conditions as to direct government influences. However, the indirect influences of the government's efforts may have been extremely important in encouraging such changes.

In the next few pages I will try to sketch out a picture of what Phu Thai village life of the past was like. Such a picture will provide a useful backdrop to highlight some of the changes which seem to have taken place in Nong Sung. Then I will describe the contemporary scene of Nong Sung as I observed it in 1962-63, noting what appear to be significant changes in social organization, and in the domains of religious, political, and economic activities. Finally, I will suggest some of the implications which might be drawn from these changes.

Any reconstruction of the Phu Thai past can be no better than the evidence on which that reconstruction is based. In this case, frankly, the evidence is spotty and sometimes of questionable validity. Despite these deficiencies, the available evidence points to certain consistent patterns in early Phu Thai life. It is this consistency which I will try to unravel from the available evidence.

The Phu Thai Past

We might roughly divide the Phu Thai past into "legend" and "history." The legend consists mainly of the stories and traditions which the Phu Thai themselves preserve of their past. The history consists of the situations and events which remain in the memories of living Phu Thai informants, the published reports of early observers of the Phu Thai, and those portions of the general history of Thailand and the Northeast that have specific relevance to the Phu Thai. The line between Phu Thai legend and history is blurred and indistinct because an important source for both is the memories of individual living Phu Thai. In part then the Phu Thai tradition blends into the historical situations and events which these individuals have experienced. Indeed, the Phu Thai legend may provide more insights into contemporary Phu Thai life than into their ancient past.

The Phu Thai Legend

The Phu Thai legend is mainly the story of how the Phu Thai happened to settle in their present locales.[3] The legendary status of this tale is indicated perhaps by the fact that it is deeply rooted in a Buddhist-defined past. For example, in the version of this story which I collected in Nong Sung, the Phu Thai were conceived to have originated in India, and the name of the Phu Thai was the result of a mispronunciation of the worlds *pu thai* (pu 'father's father') which indicated a relationship between the Phu Thai and the ancestral life of Vessantara (Phra Wetsandon), the last incarnation of the Buddha before his birth as the historic Buddha.[4]

---

[3] I have had access to a number of versions of this story other than that which I collected in Nong Sung, including a version from Renu Nakhon. There are several versions published in Thai, e.g., T. Achawan, "Prawat Phu Thai" ("History of the Phu Thai") in *Chumnum Chao Phu Thai Khrang Thi 2. B.E. 2508* (Second Meeting of the Phu Thai Association, 1965), Bangkok, Borisat Siriwat, 1965. And Phra Photthiwongsachan, "Prawat Chon Chat Phu Thai" ("History of the Phu Thai Race") in *Latthitham Mueang Tang Tang* (Beliefs and Customs of Different Peoples) Bangkok, 1963. Although there are some differences in details, there is substantial agreement between all versions I have seen.

[4] Phra Photthiwongsachan (op. cit. p. 362 f.) states that prior to their contact with Chao Anu, the King of Vientiene, the Phu Thai "still did not have religion." That is, they were "animists" at this time. Supposedly Chao Anu introduced the Phu Thai to Buddhism. Such a recent adoption of Buddhism by the Phu Thai is not unlikely.

The story recounts the various moves which Phu Thai made, from India to the Kingdom of Thaeng in the Sip Song Chau Thai region (i.e. the area around modern Dien Bien Phu), to Central Laos, and finally to Northeast Thailand. It also gives some of the reasons for these various moves and indicates some of the relationships the Phu Thai established with neighboring peoples.

According to the story, for example, the Phu Thai left the Kingdom of Thaeng after a long series of natural disasters: drought and pestilence. Chao Anu, a King of Vientiene (who reigned 1805-1825), granted the Phu Thai rights to settle in Central Laos. The Phu Thai right to this land was contested by a group of non-Buddhist hill people (*Kha*) who claimed "seniority" because of prior settlement. The Phu Thai claims were validated in a contest which they won through a bit of blatant trickery. In winning the contest the Phu Thai manifested their "moral superiority" (*bun watsana*) over the *Kha*, thus reversing the alleged seniority relationship. Some *Kha* resisted the outcome of the contest and were quickly subjugated or slaughtered.

In the Nong Sung version of this tale, there is an account of an internal struggle for leadership of the Phu Thai. Chao Kam, the leader of the Phu Thai, had a younger brother, Chao Kham, who was extremely popular. The "elder" (*phi*) feared that the "younger" (*nong*) would surpass him (literally in the story, to become "bigger than," *yai kwa*). To forestall this, the elder brother murdered the younger and after the murder he treated the people arbitrarily and with cruelty. The Phu Thai were horrified by these events, deserted Kam, and fled from Laos into Northeast Thailand to escape from the evil consequences that were sure to follow the fratricide.

Following their migration across the Mekong, the Phu Thai were granted rights to settle in the Northeast by local representatives of the Bangkok regime, such as the royal governor of Nakhon Phanom. The Phu Thai also split into the groups which formed the nucleus for the four present clusters of Phu Thai in the Northeast, each under its own local leader. One of these groups established the village of Nong Sung which was to serve as the political center for the Phu Thai of the Khamchai region until recent times. Although there are no contemporary informants who were living at the time, we might say that the Phu Thai legend ends with the establishment of Nong Sung and that Phu Thai history begins.

Phu Thai History

Phu Thai history may be reconstructed from the memories of contemporary informants, observations of the Phu Thai made in the past, such as those published by Seidenfaden, and the general history of the region.[5] The following account is a summary of these bits and pieces of evidence as they relate to Nong Sung.

Although the Phu Thai of Nong Sung acknowledged the over-lordship of the Bangkok regime, apparently they had a high degree of local autonomy. The leader of Nong Sung was designated a *chao mueang* ("leader of a domain") by the Bangkok authorities. According to contemporary informants, the Chao Mueang of Nong Sung had authority over all the Phu Thai settlements in the southern part of what is today the province of Nakhon Phanom. The Phu Thai leader may also have had jurisdiction over some non-Phu Thai Thai-Lao villages in this region as well.

The main responsibility of the Chao Mueang was to maintain order within his domain, for which he was vested with certain police and judicial powers. He was also expected to oversee the registration of all the men within his area when they reached the age of twenty. A fee was collected at this registration, part of which at least was later turned over to the Chao Mueang's immediate political superiors and ultimately to the Bangkok rulers as "tax" or "tribute."[6] Since the Chao Mueang was responsible for a fixed amount of tax, he was expected to make up any deficiencies from his own resources. Hence, failure on the part of any young man to pay his registration fee made him liable to labor on the Chao Mueang's own rice lands to compensate the Chao Mueang's expense.

While delivering the annual tribute, the Phu Thai Chao Mueang was also expected to drink the "water of allegiance" to the Thai King, symbolizing his loyalty. This water, consecrated by Brahmanist religious specialists, was supposed to choke any subordinate who falsely

---

[5] Information dealing with the early Phu Thai may be found in Phra Photthiwongsachan, op. cit. and E. Seidenfaden, "The So and Phu Thai" *Journal of the Siam Society*, Vol. 34, No. 2, pp. 145-165, 1943. Seidenfaden summarized the material on the Phu Thai in *The Thai People: Book One*, Bangkok, the Siam Society, 1958, p. 112.

[6] Aymonier, *Notes sur le Laos* (Notes on Laos), Saigon, Impremerie du Gouvernment, 1885, p. 131, reports that the tribute from Nong Sung was collected with that of Mukdahan.

swore loyalty while secretly plotting treason. Nong Sung informants, however, viewed this ceremony as an "ordeal" to demonstrate that the full tax had been paid and nothing withheld.

The Chao Mueang was the main channel of contact between the Bangkok regime and the mass of the Phu Thai. Royal officials rarely if ever penetrated into the remote Phu Thai areas. It seems that the central government put few limitations on the Chao Mueang's local authority other than those involved in the delivery of the annual tax and his pledge of allegiance to Bangkok. Despite this local autonomy, the Bangkok regime did place some restrictions on the Chao Mueang. For example, he did not have the authority to execute capital offenders. Such culprits were turned over to higher authorities for punishment. The law which the Chao Mueang administered and enforced within his domain was local customary law, not a system of national Thai law.

The Chao Mueang was recruited from the local group, purportedly by a rule of primogeniture, from the family of previous Chao Mueangs. However, the Phu Thai legend suggests that the personal qualities of the leader were also an important factor in determining authority positions, which led to the struggle between the two siblings for leadership. Apparently local political loyalties and political maneuvering were closely tied to local issues and were mediated by manipulation of the locally based kinship and marriage system. Nonetheless, the Chao Mueang was confirmed in his office by the Bangkok regime.

In discussing the era of the Nong Sung Chao Mueangs, contemporary informants often used grandiose and honorific terms which magnified their position. But it seems that the Chao Mueang's style of life did not differ strikingly from that of ordinary villagers. For example, although he controlled more land than most and had access to labor assistance through his leadership position, the Chao Mueang worked in the fields as did ordinary villagers. The Chao Mueang's house was larger and perhaps more substantially built than most village houses, but it did not differ in structure. That is, the Chao Mueang's house was not a "palace." The Chao Mueang commonly had several wives, but this was not his exclusive right. Any wealthy or powerful villager might also have several wives. The multiple marriages of the Chao Mueang may, in fact, have played an important role in the local political system by establishing strategic "alliances," but they may also have exacerbated the problems involved in succession to the Chao Mueang's position.

The symbolic focus of the Nong Sung polity was associated with veneration of local tutelary spirits, *phi pu ta* (spirits of paternal grandfather and maternal grandfather). Each village in the domain had its own set of tutelary spirits which watched over and protected the village, its lands, and people. These tutelary spirits, and hence the villages with which they were associated, were conceived to be linked together by bonds of kinship. The Chao Mueang of Nong Sung was thought to have a special relationship to the tutelary spirits of Nong Sung, who were also the "senior" spirits of the area. Thus, the Chao Mueang's special relationship to the senior spirits of the domain served, in part, to legitimize his political authority.

The Phu Thai subsistence pattern was based largely on wet-rice cultivation, supplemented by vegetable gardening and some hunting and fishing. The Phu Thai preferred to settle in a special ecological niche. They located their villages in more upland valleys than did their Thai-Lao neighbors. Cotton and silk were produced largely to meet local needs, but some of them were traded for cash. Livestock production for sale in distant markets was an important element in the early economy. Phu Thai men drove herds of livestock to markets as far away as Burma. Contemporary informants claimed that such drives might take from one to two years and were undertaken by mature men in their thirties and forties.

According to Seidenfaden, kinship considerations loomed large in early Phu Thai life. The head of a family, whether father or mother, elder brother or elder sister, was honored and obeyed. This authority was based on local customary law. In cases of adoption, a special ritual was performed to sever the relationship of the child to his/her own parents and siblings and their "ancestral spirits." After this ritual was performed, the adopted child had nothing further to do with his/her former kinsmen.

Apparently young people settled on marriage matches themselves. However, the parents of the couple worked out the actual marriage arrangements. After marriage, the young couple lived in a house built near the household of the bride's parents, although the house was built by the groom's kinsmen. Hence, a pattern of uxorilocal residence appears to have been common. Marriage involved a complex series of ceremonies extending over many years. According to Seidenfaden's reckoning, these rituals might take forty-six years to complete.

Marriage rituals consisted mainly of presentations by the groom's family of food and animals for sacrifice to the family of the bride. The aim of these ceremonies and sacrifices was to detach the girl from her ties with her parents' ancestral spirits and to link her to her husband's ancestral spirits. The structure of these rituals indicates that the relationship between a woman and her kin were regarded to be especially enduring and close. The obligation to carry out the series of marriage rituals did not cease with the death of either the bride or the groom. In the event of their early demise, the series was to be completed by their children or even grandchildren. This suggests that marriage was not simply limited to the relationship established between the individuals involved. Unfortunately, the structure of these groups is not clear from the evidence.

Indigenous beliefs about "spirits" seem to have played a very prominent role in early Phu Thai religion. For example, local political solidarity and control were linked to veneration of the village tutelary spirits mentioned above. These spirits were tied together in a sort of hierarchy establishing relationships among villages and defining the lines of the local political hierarchy. Veneration of ancestral spirits who were believed to live in and protect households was also conspicuous. As we saw, ancestral spirits were also important in the complex marriage system which Seidenfaden considered to be the most characteristic trait of the Phu Thai.

Despite the prominence of such indigenous religious elements, Buddhist monks and temples were also found in early Phu Thai villages. Celebrations such as the Buddhist "New Year" (*songkran*) were held, and Buddhist literature such as the Vessantara Jataka (Phra Wetsandon Chadok) was also present. Although Seidenfaden indicates that children were generally given no formal instruction, young men entering the monkhood probably received instruction in reading and writing Buddhist texts.

Although such Buddhist elements were present, Seidenfaden characterized the early Phu Thai as "very superstitious." Presumably he sought to emphasize the relative prominence of indigenous beliefs and practices over the Buddhist elements in early Phu Thai life. Seidenfaden also reports that during the harvest season Phu Thai youth practiced a kind of "moral laxity." He related this pattern of promiscuity to an ancient fertility cult spread widely throughout East and Southeast Asia.

Summary

Phu Thai legendary materials, the memories of individual Nong Sung informants, and early ethnographic accounts combine to present a consistent picture of the Phu Thai past. The Phu Thai formed a relatively undifferentiated and semi-autonomous ethnic enclave in Northeast Thailand, surrounded by similar but distinct Thai-Lao peoples. Such a picture is compatible with what is known of 19th and 20th century Northeast Thailand.

The main outlines of this picture might still be applied to such contemporary Phu Thai villages as Nong Sung. The Phu Thai still see themselves to be distinct from their neighbors. They still live in a special ecological niche in the uplands and follow a subsistence pattern similar to that reported for the past. Contemporary Phu Thai houses and villages seem to be basically the same as those described for an earlier era and the distinctive Phu Thai dialect is still viable.

Despite the many similarities with the Phu Thai of the past, contemporary Phu Thai have changed in various respects. Only three Phu Thai Chao Mueangs actually headed the Nong Sung domain. In the late 19th century the Bangkok government began a program of reorganization to bring the Northeastern administrative system into line with that of the Central region and to incorporate the area into the national state. According to Nong Sung informants, about 1913 the last Chao Mueang was "ordered" to move to the village of Na Kae in Nakhon Phanom province, well away from the traditional seat of his authority. The Nong Sung domain was eventually broken up into the three modern communes (*tambons*) of Khamchai, Nong Sung, and Nong Sung Tai. Each of these *tambons* is today headed by a locally elected *tambon* chief (*kamnan*) directly subordinate to the district officer (*nai amphoe*) of the Khamchai district, an official of the national bureaucracy. The transition from a semi-autonomous enclave to inclusion in the national system was accomplished more quickly on paper than in fact. It was only in 1960 that the Khamchai district that includes Nong Sung was changed from the status of sub-district (*king amphoe*) subordinate to the district officer of Mukdahan to a full-fledged district (*amphoe*).

The Phu Thai of contemporary Nong Sung are no longer simply an isolated and semi-autonomous ethnic enclave, largely because the central administration and national culture has penetrated deeply into the once remote hinterlands. The Phu Thai are increasingly becoming a part of the Thai nation. Nong Sung has become politically and economically more complex than it was in the past. Patterns of social organization and local economic, political, and religious life have been modified. Let me turn now to a description of Nong Sung as it was in 1963 to elucidate what some of these changes have been.

The Village of Nong Sung

The Village Locale

The fifteen villages which make up the *tambon* (commune) of Nong Sung are located in a triangular valley, some 193 meters above sea level. This valley is situated in the southwestern part of Khamchai district of Nakhon Phanom province. The eastern boundary of the valley is formed by a range of hills lying on the northwest to southeast axis. Another range of hills forms the southern boundary of the valley. These hills funnel a small stream, Huai Bang I, which flows in an easterly direction into the Mekong River, some 35-40 kilometers away. The valley to the north and to the west is more open.

The village of Nong Sung is situated on the banks of a small body of water (*nong*, lake or swamp) which, though very shallow in the dry season roughly from November to March, contains water all year. Nong Sung is the largest village in the *tambon* (commune) and serves as the center for the villages located in the valley.

Although Nong Sung is the *tambon* center for all villages of the *tambon*, proximity, frequent intermarriage, the pattern of land acquisition, and other factors have encouraged especially high rates of interaction between the residents of Nong Sung and three nearby villages. These villages are Nong Tae, one kilometer southeast of Nong Sung, Pa Mek, two kilometers to the south, and Nong O Yai, three kilometers due west of Nong Sung (see Map Two).[7] For some purposes these three villages might be treated as a single community.

The relations between Nong Sung and the two small villages of Nong Tae (population 390) and Pa Mek (population 125) are especially close. Neither of these villages has its own school, hence their

---

[7] Both maps in this article were originally drafted by the author and were professionally re-drawn later. Because no detailed map was available for the region around Nong Sung, he obtained dozens of aerial pictures of the Khamchai district and used them to create Map Two (footnote added by Yohko Tsuji).

children attend the Nong Sung school. Although both these villages have their own temples, frequently, as in 1963, they do not have resident monks for most of the year. Thus villagers from Nong Tae and Pa Mek make use of the Nong Sung temple and monks for their Buddhist religious activities. The larger village of Nong O Yai (population 640) is more self-sufficient in these respects.

Although several old cart tracks are still sometimes used, the main line of entrance and egress for the Nong Sung area is a precarious winding dirt road leading from the Mekong river town of Mukdahan running in a westerly direction some thirty-five kilometers to Nong Sung. This road passes through a number of villages including the villages of Nam Thiang, present site of the District Office, roughly fifteen kilometers from Nong Sung, and of Khamchai, only six kilometers from Nong Sung. The village of Khamchai had served as the *amphoe* (district) center when Khamchai was still classed as *king amphoe* (sub-district).

This main road has been open to vehicular traffic between Khamchai and Nong Sung for only a few years. Today Nong Sung is served by two busses each owned by area school teachers, one living at Nam Thiang, the other at Pa Mek. At the best of times travel on this road is never comfortable or easy, and during the rainy season motor traffic between the District Office and Nong Sung is impossible. Although there was much talk of extending the road westward to Kalasin, for practical purposes, Nong Sung was the end of the road in 1963.

The Village

Viewed from the air, Nong Sung would appear to be a collection of structures set in a sea of rice fields. The village houses might seem to huddle especially closely about the large Buddhist temple located on the bank of the lake fronting the village, for the houses in this central part of the village are packed very closely together.

Two dirt streets serve to divide the village into unequal sections. The main village street runs east-west and is simply an extension of the main road leading to the District Office and to Mukdahan. The other street runs perpendicular to the main artery, extending from the entrance of the village temple to the southern edge of the village. The two sections of the village formed by this latter street have been given official sanction, dividing the village into its two constituent "hamlets"

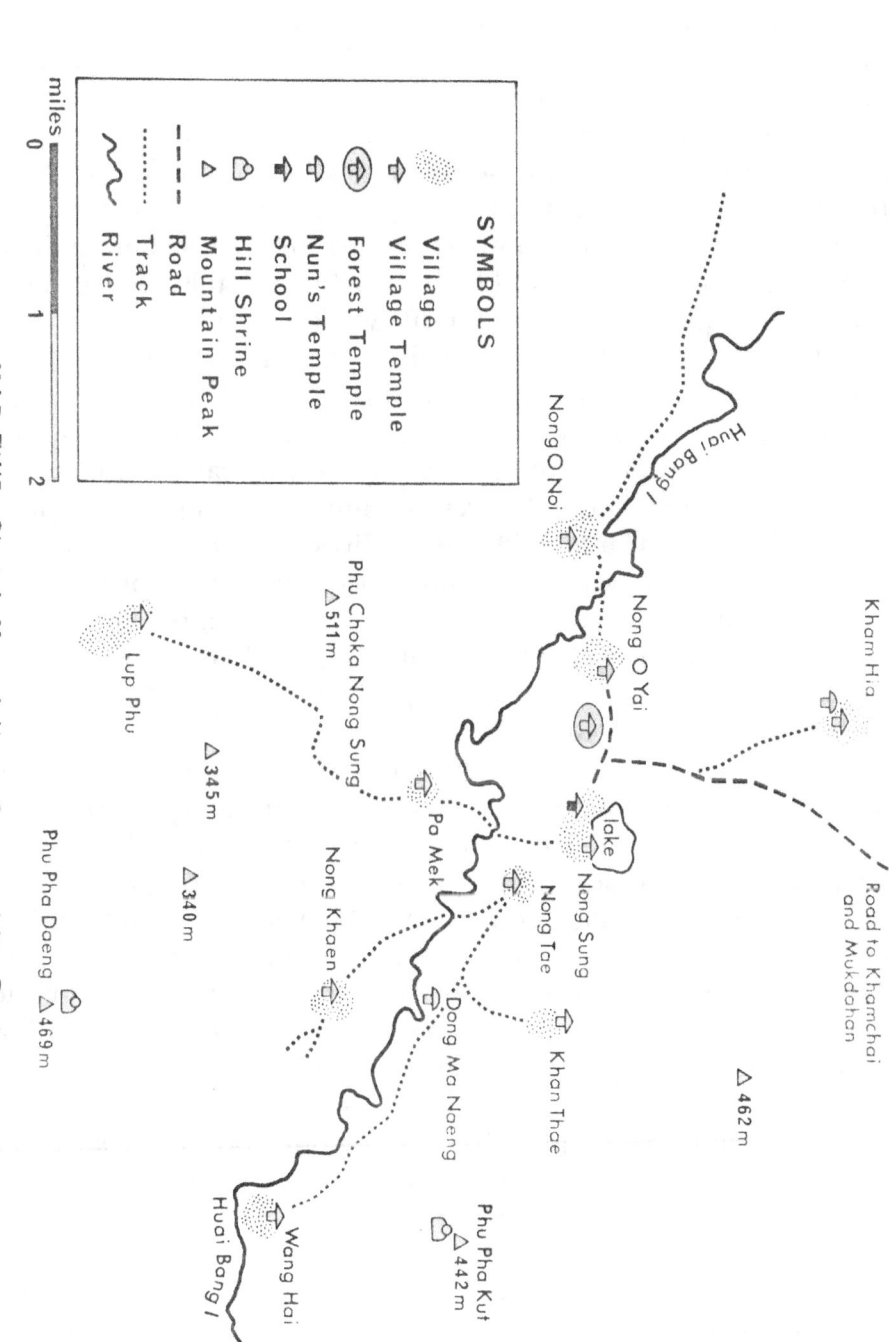

MAP TWO: Sketch Map of Nong Sung and Its Region.

(*mu*). Each hamlet has its own elected headman (*phu yai ban*). The headman of the western hamlet is traditionally, as in 1963, the *tambon* (commune) headman (*kamnan*).

Although at one time the two hamlets of Nong Sung were roughly the same size, in 1963 the western hamlet was almost twice as large as the eastern hamlet. It seems that the village has grown in recent years. However, expansion to the north is limited by the lake and to the east and south by the proximity of the rice fields and hills. Hence, most of the village expansion occurred in the western hamlet.

The western section of the village straggles out along the main village street, past a spacious yard with the two large wooden structures that make up the village school, and ends at the boundaries of a large field grown to scrub. This field, known locally as the "airfield" (*sanam bin*), now marks the western limit of Nong Sung. Villagers sometimes use this large field to graze livestock. They often complain that because it is "government land," it cannot be used for house sites, thus contributing to the crowding of the houses in the center of the village. Many villagers claimed that if the airfield were made available, many people who dislike the dense packing of houses in the center of the village would move there.

Most village houses are built of rough, locally produced planks or less frequently of woven split bamboo. Most villagers preferred a roof of corrugated iron, although many houses were roofed with thatch or home-made shingles. Houses are generally built on piles some five or six feet above the ground and entered by ladders. Commonly, the family loom, tools, pigs, chickens, and, rarely, a pony or two may be kept below such traditional-style houses. A number of more modern houses, built of plank but only a few feet above the ground and with folding doors which open up the entire front of the house, are scattered throughout the village. Such modern houses are found chiefly along the main streets and paths, and they often double as both homes and part-time stores. A very few of these houses were actually built on the ground and floored with concrete.

Although the majority of village houses are simple single story structures, there are two two-storied houses in the village. One of these is a combined home and store of the village's only full-time merchant, a Thai-born Chinese who had lived in Nong Sung for twenty-five years. The other two-storied house is the home of the village Schoolmaster, a locally born man who is also a farmer and one of the largest landholders in the village.

Kitchens are usually located in a separate structure, also built on piles, attached to the main house. Cooking is performed on a simply constructed wood-burning hearth built on a box of sand. Some more affluent villagers use stoves of molded concrete which burn charcoal. Most households also have a rice granary (*lao*) that is similar in structure to the houses, also mounted on piles, and located nearby the house. Some granaries are held in common by two or more households. Many households also own a small garden plot fenced with poles located within the village. The numerous betel nut and coconut trees scattered about the village are also owned by individuals or households.

Village Households

The co-residents of households form the basic units of Nong Sung social life. Thus, in1963, the 1417 individuals—637 males and 780 females—who made up the village population (exclusive of the monks living in the temple) were distributed throughout 232 households (*ban or huean*). As is common in villages throughout Thailand, the average age of this population is rather low; over half the villagers are nineteen years of age or younger (see Table One).

The preference of most villagers for small nucleated households is reflected in the fact that fifty-seven percent (133) of all village households are composed of only two generations, while thirty-two percent (seventy-four) of all village households contain three or more generations. The modal household size contains six residents. However, the household size ranges from a minimum of one resident (often an elderly widow living alone) to a maximum of thirteen individuals living in a household of three generations. This preference for small households is notable because it has been a contributing factor to the dense crowding in the central part of the village. Despite their complaints about such crowding of households, it is obvious that Nong Sung residents prefer having many separate but closely packed households to having fewer but multi-generational or extended family households.

Co-residents of village households are overwhelmingly close consanguineal and/or affinal kin. There are two exceptions to this

TABLE ONE

AGE AND SEX DISTRIBUTION, NONG SUNG, 1963

Age Ranges	Male		Female		Excess of Females over Males (10-Year-Age Cohorts)
0-4	111		110		
5-9	111		132		
(0-9)		(222)		(242)	20
10-14	75		86		
15-19	51		70		
(10-19)		(126)		(156)	30
20-24	45		79		
25-29	45		68		
(20-29)		(90)		(147)	57
30-34	43		52		
35-39	42		38		
(30-39)		(85)		(90)	5
40-44	26		24		
45-49	18		28		
(40-49)		(44)		(52)	8
50-54	26		26		
55-59	13		17		
(50-59)		(39)		(43)	4
60-64	17		18		
65-69	10		9		
(60-69)		(27)		(27)	--
70-74	1		9		
75-79	1		4		
(70-79)		(2)		(13)	11
80 plus	2		10		
(80 plus)		(2)		(10)	8
Total	637		780		143

general rule. One exception is the occasional "hired help" who may be brought in from outside the village and boarded during the agricultural season. A more significant exception is the young non-local school teachers who are assigned to the Nong Sung area schools. Such teachers typically establish friendly relations, often "fictive kinship" relations, with existing village households. Not uncommonly such men eventually marry girls from the local area, thereby affiliating themselves with their wife's household, or perhaps setting up a new and autonomous household. It is extremely uncommon for a man to live alone. Only one young unmarried man in the village had his own household. Even this young man did not maintain a completely autonomous household, for he ate and worked with the household of his "uncle" (his mother's brother as it happened).

Kinship and Surnames

The Nong Sung kinship system is basically a simple variant of that described for Central Thailand and the neighboring Thai-Lao. That is, kin terminology is "bilateral" and emphasizes age, sex, and genealogical distance. A few Phu Thai terms of reference are still in common use, such as *ai* for "elder male sibling" and *ueay* for "elder female sibling." These terms make a more clear-cut sexual distinction between elder siblings than Central Thai kin terms. However, the Central Thai sibling terminology, which may also have been a part of the traditional Phu Thai terminology, seems to be usurping the place of the more specialized Phu Thai forms. It is not surprising that Central Thai kinship usages are increasingly popular, for Central Thai kinship terminology forms a part of the school curriculum and one prominent visual aid in the school is a chart of Central Thai kin terms.

Seidenfaden's report suggests that kinship solidarities and obligations extending over several generations were an important part of the early Phu Thai social scene. There is little contemporary evidence that any form of unilineal extended kinship grouping ever existed in Nong Sung. However, in common with Thai throughout the nation, the Phu Thai adopted the institution of patrilineally inherited surnames (*nam sakun*) following an order issued by the King (Rama VI) in 1916. Although many older village residents, especially women, displayed some uncertainty and confusion about their own surnames, this institution has been readily adopted by Nong Sung villagers.

Informants claimed that when surnames were first introduced to Nong Sung, only four names were adopted by the entire village population. These four surnames are now represented in over one-half of the present village households. Phu Thai women are usually known by their husband's surname after marriage. In 1963 there were forty-two distinct surnames represented in Nong Sung.

The large number of distinct surnames currently found in the village provides some measure of the marriage of men into the community from outside. Certain surnames are associated with specific villages in the locality, thus providing a clue to the pattern of intermarriage in the area. But some locally born men had simply adopted a new surname for any of a variety of reasons: they liked the sound of a new surname better than their old name; they did not get along with their paternal relatives.

While sharing a common surname may be a badge of affiliation and friendship in individual cases, persons sharing a common surname do not form a corporate group, have no mutual obligations or duties, nor do they act in concert on any occasions. Furthermore, sharing a common surname is not a bar to marriage. Incest rules apply primarily only to the most immediate circle of kinsmen. Marriages between "first cousins," who are "siblings" in the local terminology, are not unknown and under certain conditions may be thought desirable. For example, a first cousin may be favored as a second spouse for a widow or widower with children.

Marriage

Household units are maintained or established anew through marriage and a process of throwing off nuclear family units from a core parental household. Most village marriages are formed through romantic attachments between the young couple themselves. Commonly after the couple have agreed to marry, the girl will consult a local "seer" (*mo du*) about the auspiciousness of the match. If the match is held to be appropriate, a "go-between" (*lam* or *thao kae*), usually a respected elderly villager, is called in to work out the details of the marriage between the parents of the couple. Such details include the determination of "bride-price" or *kha dong*, which refers literally to the cost of establishing the *dong* or "in-law relationship" between the respective sets of parents, as well as the respective contributions each set of parents will make in setting up the young couple after marriage.

Although no coercion is used, arranged marriages sometimes occur. Arranged marriages most commonly involve individuals with some physical defect (e.g. lameness) or some personality problem, most notably girls with "domineering" personalities who frighten village men away from marriage. Mothers are also believed to encourage particular matches between their children and other village youth. If parental objection to a match proposed by a young couple should arise, the young people may simply elope, returning after the *fait accompli* to request and usually to receive the parental blessings.

Marriage and Alternative Roles

As noted earlier, before agreeing to a marriage, young girls commonly consult a local "seer" about the auspiciousness of the match. Men rarely consult seers on such matters. This implies that women manifest a special concern about marriage by resorting to these ritual consultations. Such special concern of women points up a feature of the contemporary, and perhaps the historic, situation with respect to marriage. Women have only one career open to them, that of wife and mother. Men on the other hand have a variety of roles available to them which may lead them to postpone or perhaps to totally avoid marriage. For example, men may tour about the country for fun (called locally *pai din*, in the equivalent of the Central Thai *pai thiao*), seeking out part or full time work away from the village. They may also choose to continue their education or even to enter the monkhood.

Many of these alternative roles open to men involve leaving the village, for a time at least, perhaps never to return. The age distribution of the contemporary village population (see Table One above) indicates that men take advantage of these possibilities. Thus, there are 147 women but only ninety men in the age cohort of 20-29 years living in the village. Many marriages take place between people in this age range, but men in this age group are in short supply. Hence, the concern which women express in ritual consultations may be well founded, for marriage seems to have different implications for women than for men. Other factors, such as conceptions about the permanence or impermanence of marriage, may also make a contribution to this concern.

The notion that marriage has qualitatively different implications

TABLE TWO

AGE AT FIRST MARRIAGE, 204 COUPLES, NONG SUNG, 1963

Age at Marriage	Number of Men	Number of Women
15	1	6
16	4	8
17	3	18
18	9	29
19	11	34
20	24	23
21	13	21
22	22	18
23	18	11
24	13	8
25	20	5
26	14	5
27	15	7
28	7	-
29	7	4
30	4	4
31	6	1
32	4	-
33	2	1
34	1	-
35	3	1
36	2	-
:	:	:
:	:	:
45	1	-
Total	204	204

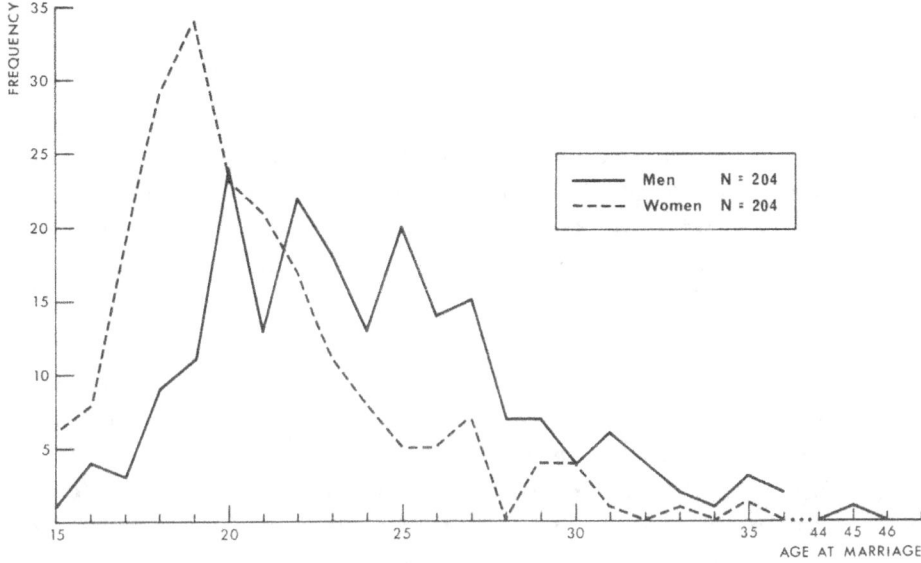

CHART ONE: Age at First Marriage, 204 Couples, Nong Sung (1963)

for men and for women is supported by the distribution of age at first marriage for 204 Nong Sung couples (see Table Two and Chart One). The distribution of age at marriage for the 204 women is unimodal and sharply peaked about the age of nineteen years, while median age is twenty years. The comparable distribution for men peaks at about age twenty but is multimodal and considerably flatter than the distribution of women's ages at marriage. The median age of the men's distribution is twenty-four years. If marriage carried the same implications for men and for women, we would expect that these distributions would parallel each other more closely than they do. Basically these distributions reflect the differences in role alternatives open to men and to women.[8]

Divorce and Separation

On marriage a bridegroom typically moves into the household of his bride's parents for a time. The actual time which the young couple spends in the parents' household varies widely, but it is not

[8] It seems likely that such differences in the distributions of ages at marriage for men and for women are extremely common. However, these differences, in conjunction with the population figures for Nong Sung, spell out the special pressures on women with respect to marriage under contemporary conditions.

uncommon for them to stay until the birth of their first child. This early period of marriage seems to be particularly important, for most separations and divorces occur during this time if they are to occur at all.

Informants sometimes express the view that marriage ties are brittle. Other than gossip there are few sanctions applied when a marriage does break up. Indeed, there is an explicit belief that men are more ready to "throw away" (*thing pai*)—separate from or divorce their spouses and children, if any—than are women. It is difficult to determine if the actual rate of separation or divorce justifies the view that marriage ties are fragile, or if, in fact, men initiate such separations more frequently than do women. The pattern of men moving into the wives' parents' household for a period immediately after marriage might well encourage the impression that husbands initiate such separations more frequently than do wives. At any rate, in 1963 there were twenty men and nine women currently married who had had one or more previous marriages disrupted by separation or divorce. There were also six men and eleven women currently separated from their spouses with the strong probability that such separation would continue.

Marriage and Movement

Of the 232 marriages for which I had adequate data, the majority (six-three percent or 145) involved a man and a woman who had both been born and raised in Nong Sung. That is, these marriages were "village endogamous." In the remaining marriages, at least one partner (both in two cases) was born and raised outside the village. Of these latter marriages, the overwhelming majority of the non-village spouses moved into the village from nearby localities, i.e., from villages within the Khamchai district. That is, of the eighty-eight marriage partners recruited from outside the village, thirteen men and forty-seven women had been born and raised within the Khamchai district.

It is difficult to gather comparable data with respect to individuals born in the village but marrying outside the village. I recorded the cases of some seventeen men and forty-one women who had left the village and were *known* to have married elsewhere within the district. These figures taken in conjunction with those for marriages into the village might suggest that some sort of stable relationship exists between the numbers of men and the numbers of women marrying into and out of the village. Such a view might be misleading, for if we were to include in these figures all the men and all the women who had moved temporarily or permanently from the village for *any* reason and whose marital status was not definitely known, we would add a further forty-four men to the total, but only fourteen women. Once more, these figures reflect the differences in role alternatives between men and women which we also saw in the village population figures. As a generalization, however, it is safe to say that movement into or out of the village by a woman is almost invariably due to marriage considerations. Men may move into or away from the village for a variety of reasons, only one of which is marriage.

Affiliation Within and Between Households

Despite the general preference for nucleated and autonomous households, there are actually a number of special ties of affiliation of nuclear units both within and between households. Although commonly only a temporary affiliation, the custom of men living in their bride's parental household is one such tie. Access to rice lands is a basic factor influencing final decisions of where to locate and affiliate young nuclear families. In the absence of other stable sources of income (e.g. school teachers' salaries), rice land provides the economic base which permits the maintenance and eventual autonomy of households. Access to such land is obtained basically by affiliating the young nuclear family with an older household of parental generation and working land in common with the older household. Over time the young nuclear family is given increasing control over specific parcels of land and eventually "ownership" of these lands. Thus, the holdings of parental households tend to diminish as their children and their children's spouses form new nuclear families and establish the core for a new autonomous household. Hence, the notion of an "estate" to be kept intact and passed on to descendents is not a feature of contemporary Nong Sung life.

A number of factors influence decisions concerning where to finally locate and affiliate the younger nuclear family *vis-à-vis* parental generation households. Some of these factors are: the relative availability of land from *either* (or possibly both) the husband's and the wife's parental household (or kinsmen), the number, age, and sex of

TABLE THREE

AFFILIATION WITHIN AND BETWEEN HOUSEHOLDS, NONG SUNG, 1963

Affiliation	Within Household	Between Households	Total
Virilateral	57	23	80
Uxorilateral	13	13	26
	—	—	—
Total	70	36	106

siblings of either the husband or the wife who might also make claims on the respective parental households, the decisions which such siblings may have already made in this respect, the relative statuses and reputations of the respective parental households, and such even more intangible factors as compatibility between the members of the younger family and the respective parental households. In particular cases any and/or all of these factors may play a decisive role in determining the affiliation of a younger nuclear family with an older established household. Note, however, that direct affiliations of nuclear households of the same generation without a connecting link of an older generational household are extremely rare.

We may distinguish two modes of affiliation between nuclear families in Nong Sung. One mode of affiliation is sharing a common residence and working land in common. This might be called affiliation *within* a household. The other mode of affiliation involved maintaining separate residences, but working land in common. This mode of affiliation might be called affiliation *between* households. In either case, the pattern of affiliation in contemporary Nong Sung is overwhelmingly virilateral, rather than uxorilateral. That is, affiliation is more frequently through the husband and his kinsmen than through the wife and her kinsmen. Thus, within multigenerational households virilateral affiliation is more than four times as frequent as uxorilateral affiliation. Between households, virilateral affiliation is almost twice as frequent as uxorilateral affiliation (see Table Three).

This pattern of virilateral affiliation is striking because Seidenfaden's report on the early Phu Thai indicates that a pattern of uxorilocal residence was common, hence perhaps a pattern of uxorilateral affiliation also existed. The tendency towards virilateral affiliation is also interesting from the perspective of the contemporary marriage system, which leads men to live for a time with the household of the bride's parents. We might expect that this situation would tend to bias affiliation more in the direction of uxorilateral affiliation rather than virilateral affiliation. Apparently it does not.

Household Heirship

The affiliation of young nuclear families is further complicated by the problem of disposing of parents' houses. As we observed, parents' landholdings tend to diminish as control over their land is taken on by those of their children and their children's spouses who have chosen to affiliate with them. Thus, in the normal course of events the parental estate is largely "residual." But parents' house forms an important part of their estate, and it cannot be parceled out as can land. However, by the time parents retire from active life or die, a putative heir to their house and his or her nuclear family is commonly already in residence in the household. The rights of this putative heir to the parental house have already been validated by living and working in common with the parents over a period of years. Thus, the putative heir is already in possession. It would be most unusual for a sibling to contest the rights of this putative heir to the parental house.

The evidence I gathered on household heirship in Nong Sung indicates that no simple principle of sex of child or birth order, or a combination of these, determines household heirship. However, as the situation with respect to affiliations within and between households might suggest, the probability is greater that such an heir will be a son rather than a daughter. There is also a tendency for elder sons to be heirs rather than younger sons.

The tendency towards a virilateral and "male" bias with respect to affiliation between nuclear units and household heirship is interesting for several reasons. For one thing, the situation in Nong Sung contrasts with that frequently reported for the Thai-Lao. In Thai-Lao villages it is common to find affiliation and heirship biased in an uxorilateral "female" direction. Aside from the contrast with the Thai-Lao, the circumstances in contemporary Nong Sung also appear to contrast with the situation reported for the early Phu Thai.

Early Phu Thai marriage ritual indicated a close attachment between a woman and her parental family. Hence a complex series of rituals were necessary in order to sever her links with the ancestral spirits of her parents and to attach her to the ancestral spirits of her husband. The report that the young couple lived in a household near that of the girl's parents is consistent with the marriage ritual. On marriage then, a man moved near his wife's family, a pattern of uxorilocal residence. This situation suggests that a concomitant pattern of uxorilateral affiliation between households may also have been common. As we noted, such a pattern is not particularly unusual, for many contemporary Thai-Lao villages manifest such a pattern. However consistent and plausible Seidenfaden's report may be concerning the early Phu Thai, the contemporary patterns of residence, affiliation, and heirship in Nong Sung differ strikingly.

Perhaps more interestingly, the actual situation in Nong Sung appears to conflict with a formulation of Phu Thai "rules of inheritance" offered by contemporary informants. Stated baldly, this formulation is that: "Men inherit rice lands; women inherit houses." Given our reconstruction of the Phu Thai past, such a "rule" has some plausibility, for it is consistent with early Phu Thai marriage practices in which women remained near their parents and men moved on marriage. We might conceptualize the implications of the stated rule in the following way: men circulated through households while possessing rice lands; women (or their work) circulated through rice lands while possessing households. Whatever the historical situation may actually have been, it seems clear that the inheritance rule stated by contemporary informants does not account for the present situation. Today, men are more likely to obtain both rice lands and households.

At first glance, the contemporary situation might suggest a simple "reversal" of the former Phu Thai pattern. Whereas formerly women were attached to their parental families and men thus had to move and affiliate with the household of their wife's parents, today it is men who are closely tied to their parental households and women must move and affiliate with the household of their husbands' parents. Be that as it may, the situation in contemporary Nong Sung is more complex than a simple reversal of the old pattern; it is something new.

Under the early Phu Thai pattern, women remained fixed and

men moved. If there were a simple reversal of this pattern, men would remain fixed and women would move. If we limited ourselves to the data respecting the individuals actually living in the village in 1963, such a reversal of pattern might seem to be borne out. However, such a procedure would exclude other data concerning individuals born in Nong Sung but not residing in the village in 1963. For example, we observed that men have access to a variety of roles which women generally do not. Many of the roles open to men involve movement outside the village. The dearth of men in the age cohort of 20-29 years suggests that village men do, in fact, take advantage of these alternatives. In short, Nong Sung men do not remain fixed. They are even more mobile than women though their reasons and locations of movement are different from those for women.

It seems clear that the close attachment that once existed between a woman and her parental family and was reflected in past marriage rituals has been, in some fashion, undermined. Women are no longer so closely tied to their parental households. Obviously the relationship of women to her husband has become increasingly important at the expense of her attachment to her parental family. Maybe, this situation has been encouraged by the dearth of men in the strategic age cohort which makes men of this age "scarce goods" on the marriage market. However, it is by no means clear that a correspondingly close tie of solidarity between men and their parental families has developed. Adoption of the institution of patrilineally inherited surnames might encourage such a development, but there is little evidence of any close knit bonds of male solidarity.

Perhaps some of the factors that will elucidate these changes in Nong Sung social life will be revealed by a discussion of other realms of contemporary village life.

Religion in Nong Sung

Statements of contemporary Nong Sung informants and reports of early observers indicate that indigenous "animistic" elements were extremely prominent in early Phu Thai religion although Buddhist elements were also to be found on the village scene. These indigenous elements were especially prominent in two spheres of life with political relevance: veneration of local tutelary spirits and the marriage system associated with concern for ancestral spirits. There is some reason to believe that these two spheres were also closely related under the conditions of early Phu Thai life.

Today, Nong Sung religion is dominated by Buddhist and Buddhist related "Brahmanistic" beliefs and practices. Indigenous elements (e.g., concern with "spirits") assume an almost residual character. Some indigenous religious practices, such as the "moral laxity" at harvest time reported by Seidenfaden, have completely disappeared. When contemporary villagers speak or act "religiously," they invariably speak and act within a Buddhist framework. This includes their references to the past. Hence, as noted earlier, the Phu Thai legend is rooted in a Buddhist past.

The temporal and spatial dimensions of Nong Sung life are imbedded in a matrix of Buddhist symbols, acts, and beliefs. The daily round begins with the passage of monks through the village accepting offerings of food from householders. The monthly and yearly cycles are marked off on the Buddhist lunar calendar and by periodic Buddhist ceremonies, such as the bi-monthly "Sabbath" (*wan phra*), or annual ceremonies, such as that honoring Phra Wetsandon (*bun phra wet*). Entire seasons are invested with Buddhist significance. A good example of this is the Buddhist "Lent" (*phansa*) during which young village men may enter the monkhood for a time.

Statues of the Buddha arranged on household altars and ubiquitous pictures of the Emerald Buddha or the King serving as a monk (distributed by the national government) bring Buddhist symbols directly into the household. Regional and national objects, localities, and events are the subjects of local religious interest. Thus, in 1963, a busload of villagers went to the famous nearby temple of That Phanom during the celebration of the Buddhist "All Saints Day" (*makha bucha*), a festival which attracts pilgrims from all over Thailand and Laos.

Even the untamed hills and forests surrounding the village have been penetrated by Buddhist objects and symbols. Statues of the Buddha and other shrines dot the hills overlooking the village. Such shrines, commonly erected by some devout laymen, may serve as the focus for pilgrimages by villagers.

There is a "forest temple" (*wat pa*) located in the forest between Nong Sung and Nong O Yai to the west. This temple is inhabited by monks belonging to the Thammayut order of the Thai Monkhood.

(The monks of the Thammayut order adhere to a more strict interpretation of the monastic discipline than the larger Mahanikai branch of the Thai monkhood.) Although such forest temples do not "belong" to any village, this temple was built in 1940-41 on land donated by a prosperous Nong Sung villager, by local labor, and with local resources. The monks of this temple pass through Nong Sung each morning gathering alms, and thus serve as a focus for Buddhist ritual activities.

Of course, the village temple and its resident monks, who are of the Mahanikai branch of monks, are the most concrete manifestations of the penetration of Buddhism within Nong Sung. The temple is the largest, most elaborate set of structures in the village and is the only edifice constructed of permanent materials (i.e., brick, stone, and mortar) rather than wood or bamboo. Villagers invest the temple with an aura of permanence which characterizes no other institution in the village. Indeed, the temple might be taken as the symbolic mooring place for the sentiments of all villagers, for a village without a temple and resident monks is thought to be "incomplete." One indication of the special role the temple plays in village life is that, with the possible exception of the village school, the temple is virtually the single village institution which can mobilize the activities of the entire village.

The capacity of the temple to mobilize the entire village was particularly apparent in 1963, for the village undertook two projects to improve the temple. One project was the construction of a "hall of the water" (*sala nam*) built on piles in the lake fronting the temple. The aim of this project was to provide a comfortable place for the monks to study during the hottest part of the year. The other project, initially a modest attempt to strengthen the foundations of the temple's sanctuary (*bot* or locally *sim*), took on larger proportions when it was decided to rebuild the sanctuary from the ground up.

At some time or other over a period of several months, virtually the entire village population was involved in one or both projects. Even the children made a contribution. One day the Schoolmaster and teachers led the children to a nearby dry stream bed gathering stones to be used in reinforcing the sanctuary's foundation. Although both projects were begun in early 1963, neither was completed by the end of the year when I left the village. The two projects strained local resources too far, and plans to obtain outside assistance were being discussed. To seek government aid for the completion of these projects, the Schoolmaster, in particular, was trying to use his connections in the Ministry of Education in Bangkok, which includes the Department of Religious Affairs.

All villagers identify themselves as Buddhists, but there is a wide range of sophistication among them with respect to their individual understanding of Buddhist doctrines. Although esoteric Buddhist beliefs are learned and preached by local monks, most villagers are linked more closely to the system of Buddhist rituals rather than to sophisticated doctrines. It is within Buddhist ritual contexts that villagers most clearly display their Buddhist commitments. In Nong Sung Buddhist ritual is called *ao bun* (literally "to take merit"), a form parallel in usage to the Central Thai *tham bun* ("to make merit"). For villagers the aim of Buddhist ritual is to accumulate "merit" (*bun*), to earn a sojourn in "paradise" (*sawan*) for a time after death, or to gain an enhanced status in a future life on earth. Villagers thus display their commitment to Buddhist beliefs and values within ritual contexts.

In the eyes of villagers, Buddhist rituals do more than accumulate religious merit that will influence future lives. Persistent performance of such rituals is also thought to develop good moral characteristics in the individual. This is one reason why many routine Buddhist rituals, such as feeding the monks, are commonly left in the hand of women, for women "need" to develop these good habits more than do men. Common participation and involvement in Buddhist rituals is also thought to create enduring moral bonds between individuals. Hence, the major units and grouping which make up Nong Sung social life are revealed in Buddhist ritual performances.

The central importance of the household unit in village life is indicated in the daily ritual of feeding the monks. Although women actually prepare the food and offer it to the monks as they pass through the village each morning, the offering is not simply an individual act. In this context women are representatives of their households, for the resources given to the monks are the fruit of the common efforts of the household as a unit.

"Household merit-making" ceremonies (*ao bun huean*) involve not only the sponsoring household but also include the informal social network within which the members of the household are enmeshed. A household invites a number of the monks to come to their house for an evening to chant and to pray. The following morning the monks return to pray once more and are offered food. Such rituals are never restricted exclusively to the sponsoring household members. Neighbors, kinsmen, and friends are invited to participate, to contribute to feeding the monks, and to share in the religious rewards stemming from the ritual. Thus, household merit-making ceremonies display the ties which bind household members to others in the community.

The entire community may jointly participate in other Buddhist rituals. During the Buddhist Lent a number of such ceremonies take place. The ceremony of "decorating the earth" (*bun khao pradap din*) is concerned, in part, with the prosperity of the coming agricultural year, and the "gods" (*thewada*) and the "souls of the deceased" (*winyan*) are invited to participate along with the villagers. On the day the ceremony is held, virtually the entire village assembles in the temple yard. They form a circle, not in household groups, but roughly according to age and sex, and each individual makes an offering of food to the monks. A huge amount of food is given to the monks during the ceremony. However, the food is then eaten in concert by the monks and the villagers in the large "assembly hall" (*sala wat*) of the temple. This ritual thus displays the individual and the collective commitments of villagers to Buddhist institutions and values.

Another communal ritual is the Kathin ceremony which was sponsored by the people of Nong Sung in 1963. Indeed, the Kathin took on the attributes of an official community function, for the decision to hold a Kathin was made by the leading members of the community, while the goods which were to be offered were collected over a period of several weeks at the house of the *tambon* (commune) headman. A large collection of monk's robes, alms bowls, paper, pencils, and other paraphernalia useful to monks was gathered. On the appointed day, the entire village, both adults and children, formed a raucous procession. It descended on the nearby forest temple which had been selected as the object of the ceremony. After circling the assembly hall of the forest temple three times, the villagers presented the goods to the resident monks.

As performed in the Nong Sung area, the Kathin ceremony invariably involves choosing a temple other than that of the sponsoring village to be the object of the ceremony. In this case, the offering was made to the forest temple which is not attached to any village. Some time later the Nong Sung temple was the object of a Kathin ceremony sponsored by a nearby village.

The focus of the Kathin ceremony on a non-local temple makes evident the trans-local element implicit in all Buddhist rituals. Buddhist beliefs and values are not limited to kin groups, to villages, or to localities. They are thought to be universal and to apply to all mankind. Indeed, Buddhist belief extends beyond man to embrace all sentient life including not only animals, but also "gods," the "souls of the deceased," "spirits," and "demons" (*pret*). Villagers' participation in Buddhist rituals and their adherence to Buddhist values link them with a diffusely-defined and open-ended Buddhist moral community that transcends their everyday experiences and local ties. Thus, villagers' loyalty to the temple is first as a Buddhist institution and only secondly as a village institution.

Buddhist ceremonies, such as that honoring Phra Wetsandon (*bun phra wet*), and numerous temple fairs attract huge crowds from a wide area who are eager to make merit and enjoy themselves in the process. In addition, as we noted above, villagers also participate in regional and national ceremonies. Hence, Buddhist commitments unite people of Nong Sung with a much broader community of fellow believers. By identifying themselves with such a supra-local symbolic order, villagers are, to some extent, freed from their dependence on particularistic local symbols and attachments.

Buddhist rituals separate individuals from their particularistic attachments more explicitly than by simply defining a loose moral community with which individuals identify. Entering the monkhood, which is thought to be one of the most meritful things a man can do, illustrates this point. In the ritual of becoming a monk, the candidate gives up his attachments to parents and kinsmen, to friends and girlfriends, and to the ordinary village style of life. This transition is symbolized by shaving his head, by donning the yellow robe, and by assuming a new religious name. The new monk follows an "extraordinary" style of life by subordinating himself to the 227 rules of the monastic discipline, which govern the monk's every act and effectively cut him off from the kinds of activities most village men enjoy, snacking at all hours and teasing girls, for instance. Indeed, villagers view the monk's style of life to be no easy one.

It is because the monastic life is so difficult that villagers automatically grant all monks special marks of extreme deference and respect for symbolizing the truth of Buddhist beliefs. Monks bridge the gap between the abstract moral order and everyday life. Service as a monk is more than highly regarded; there is an explicit ideal that every man should spend at least a portion of his life, commonly one Lenten season, as a member of the Buddhist Order or Sangha. Therefore, service as a monk has a social value as well as a religious value. Nonetheless, it seems that this ideal has never been perfectly fulfilled. (If it were, it would probably not be a very good idea.) Only residents of fifty-six percent (131) of all village households had, at least minimally, met this ideal.

It is not only the young man who gives up his attachments to his kinsmen on entering the monkhood, for as part of the ordination ritual, his parents explicitly give up their claims on him as well. In fact, there is a popular belief that most of the merit stemming from a young man's ordination goes to his mother because she gives up her claim on him. Since women can not be monks, having a son enter the monkhood is an especially important source of religious rewards for women. Hence, some young men actually enter the monkhood for the sake of their mothers.

The commitments of villagers to Buddhist values encourage them to symbolically "give up" their kin ties and attach themselves to an overriding Buddhist moral order and to Buddhist institutions. Such symbolic acts of renunciation may enhance the nucleated structure of the village family and a highly "individualistic" mode of life in two ways: first, by enticing the individual out of his nuclear family and projecting him into a universalistic Buddhist-defined social realm that transcends kinsmen, locality, and the rural style of life; second, by communicating to the individual that his ultimate interests are not irrevocably linked to his particularistic attachments but perhaps away from them.

It is clear that monks play a particularly important role in village Buddhism, for they serve as the primary focus of Buddhist ritual activities and stand as the most proximate and potent symbols of the Buddhist-defined order. But the monkhood is more than a collection of individuals; it is an organization, the Sangha, which is also a potent religious symbol for villagers. Although the organization of the Buddhist Order is not especially tight, it extends from the most remote rural village into the highest reaches of the national society. Indeed, we might say that the Sangha is the skeleton that gives shape to the diffuse Buddhist moral community, because the Sangha and its constituent monks are the objects of universal reverence and respect.

A monk may find a place to stay in any temple in the Kingdom, assured of sufficient food and a position of high respect. And monks are inveterate travelers, except during the Lenten season when they must remain in a single temple. Thus temple populations may vary widely due to the influx of young men during the Lenten season and this proclivity of monks for traveling about from temple to temple.

The monastic institution eases geographic mobility among its members, who are, after all, recruited from the mass of ordinary villagers. Hence, the monkhood serves to redistribute a part of the rural population. In 1963, for example, there were seven men of varying ages who had initially come to Nong Sung from outside the district as monks, eventually leaving the monkhood and settling permanently in the village. It is more difficult to determine precisely how many men had permanently left the village and settled elsewhere through the monastic channel. But in 1963, there were at least five young men from Nong Sung serving as monks in urban temples, perhaps never to return.

The monkhood encourages social mobility as well as geographic mobility. Men who have served as monks may be addressed by honorific titles signifying either the monastic rank earned by passing national examinations of religious knowledge or the length of time served in the Order. Some men in Nong Sung had acquired various skills or knowledge (e.g. curing lore, astrological knowledge), which earned both special respect and a small income in the community.

Today, ecclesiastical advancement may be more important than ever before. It is possible for village men who, for one reason or another, are cut off from advanced education in the national school system to acquire advanced education in temple schools that range up to the Buddhist universities located in Bangkok. Thus, service as a monk may become a vehicle for advancement in both the local community and in the national society.

If Buddhism is the most prominent feature of contemporary Nong Sung religion, what has become of the indigenous elements that loomed so large with respect to marriage and local political solidarity in early Phu Thai religious life? Modern Nong Sung religious practice indicates that indigenous beliefs about spirits have been deeply eroded.

We saw earlier that village girls often seek the advice of a local "seer" (*mo du*) concerning the appropriateness of a proposed marriage match. Seers also specify an auspicious date and time for weddings and other ceremonies to take place. Given the psychological tensions associated with marriage in Nong Sung (e.g. the importance of marriage as a sole career for women, the scarcity of men, the brittleness of marriage), seers serve to legitimize particular marriage matches and perform a largely "therapeutic" function. The paraphernalia and techniques which seers use are commonly based on horoscopes and astrological knowledge derived from non-indigenous, i.e. Buddhist-Brahamistic, lore. Seers are not, in any simple fashion, an outgrowth or elaboration of an *indigenous* Phu Thai religion.

Although Buddhism is prominent in Nong Sung religion, there is no specifically Buddhist wedding ceremony. In fact, monks never even attend weddings in Nong Sung, but young couples commonly take care to jointly feed the monks on their wedding day or shortly after. (This is one of the few occasions when men customarily feed monks.) In addition, ancestral spirits are also not a prominent consideration in contemporary marriage practices. Today, beliefs about the "soul elements" (*khwan*) of the couple involved are the central focus of the marriage ceremony.

Each individual is thought to have a number of "soul elements." Conventionally there are thirty-six "soul elements," each associated with a sense organ, such as "soul of the eye" (*khwan ta*), "soul of the mouth" (*khwan pak*), and so on. These elements are only loosely integrated in the individual and have a tendency to drift out of equilibrium with great ease. This disequilibrium may lead to illness or perhaps to personality disorganization. The problem is met through performance of a very common and general ritual, "tying the soul elements" (*su khwan*). The ceremony basically consists of the officiant praying to recall the wondering "soul elements" back to the individual and then fastening them firmly to his or her body. This is symbolized by tying a bit of string around the wrist.

There are certain "soul-tying doctors" (*mo su khwan*) who are thought to be especially efficacious in this technique. Such men, as well as "seers," commonly acquire their special skill in Buddhist contexts, often while serving in the monkhood. Thus, such practitioners are typically men and highly respected in the community.

The "soul-tying" ceremony is so simple and widely known it may be performed by virtually anyone. The ritual is commonly resorted to in cases of illness, on important occasions in the life of individuals (e.g. before ordination, on entering the army or leaving the village on an extended trip), and on occasions of special community importance (e.g. when a high official visits he may be ceremonially "tied" to the village). The wedding ceremony is basically a "tying the soul elements" ritual.

Wedding ceremonies are usually performed by some highly respected villager, preferably the highest status person available. The officiant first ties the "soul elements" of the groom and of the bride to their bodies individually. Then the wrists of the young couple are tied together, symbolizing their union, while the officiant prays that their "soul elements" stay bound together. Guests at the wedding may also tie the wrists of the young couple, and at the conclusion of the ceremony their wrists may be a mass of white strings. The ceremony concludes with a feast participated in by the couple, their guests, and kinsmen. In present day ceremonies preceding a wedding and in the wedding ceremony itself, the central focus of attention is not ancestral spirits, but the characteristics of the couple involved.

The symbolic focus of early Phu Thai political solidarity was linked with a system of village tutelary spirits (*phi pu ta*), which were ordered in some sort of hierarchy of "seniority." A simple wooden shed located in a small lane next to the village school served as the "shrine" (*ho*) of Nong Sung's tutelary spirits. In the year that I lived in the village, no offerings nor ceremonies were held to honor these spirits. The guardian of this shrine (*chao phi pu ta*) is an elderly villager who was, before his retirement, the official "commune doctor" (*phaet pracham tambon*). This man admitted that an annual ceremony should be held to "feed" these spirits (*liang phi pu ta*) but, in fact such a ceremony had not been held in several years. He remarked that the villagers were not particularly concerned with tutelary spirits. He ventured the opinion that if some disaster, an epidemic or a drought, for example, were to strike the village, a ceremony seeking the benevolent interest and assistance of the tutelary spirits might be held. Even the guardian of the tutelary spirits shrine was not particularly interested in the spirits. It seems clear that whatever importance the tutelary spirits might once have had in Nong Sung life, today, their influence is dissipated, and these figures are now largely ignored. (However, in nearby villages, such as Nong O Yai, tutelary spirits are considerably more prominent than in Nong Sung.) Today, the focus of political activity in Nong Sung centers on the village school where national symbols are displayed, and on the village temple which is tied to the national Sangha.

Nonetheless, concern with "spirits" is by no means absent from contemporary Nong Sung life. Every villager, including monks, agrees that spirits "exist" and can not simply be ignored because, for example, spirits may sometimes cause illness. However, today many beliefs about spirits are closely articulated with Buddhist and Brahamnistic practices and beliefs. Thus, spirit attacks can be forestalled or countered by the prayers of monks who may effectively exorcise spirits through the power of Buddhist symbols. Disequilibrium of an individual's "soul elements" may make him particularly susceptible to spirit attack. Under these circumstances the patient may be treated by a ceremony "tying the soul elements." Note that neither monks nor "soul-tying doctors" propitiate spirits. They both stand in opposition to and counterattack against the spirits.

There are, however, a number of "spirit doctors" (*mo yao*) who mediate more directly and benignly between men and spirits. Spirit doctors communicate directly with the spirit world through a "familiar spirit" (*yao*) which has attached itself to the spirit doctor. Spirit doctors are able to discover what spirit is causing the illness, why the spirit is displeased, and what offering the spirit will accept to desist. Most spirit doctors are women, and they are frequently thought to inherit their familiar spirit from some close kinsmen. The position of spirit doctor is not particularly respected, and their services are generally sought out as a last resort after other practitioners have been unable to cure a patient.

Viewing contemporary religious practice in Nong Sung against the backdrop of early Phu Thai religion, it is clear that some striking changes have taken place. Indigenous practices and beliefs have been swamped by non-indigenous religious elements. In particular, village religion has become increasingly "Buddha-ized." The pervasive penetration of Buddhist beliefs and practices on the village scene seems to have come about unconsciously and largely through local initiatives, although no doubt the national government has provided a climate conducive to such changes.

The precise details of this shift in village religion are lost to history. However, given the initial acceptance of Buddhism on the local scene, the structure of Buddhism makes these changes understandable. No matter how unsophisticated rural monks may be, they are taught at least a basic orthodoxy, which they may use to "reinterpret" local beliefs to bring them into line with Buddhist beliefs. Of course, in such a situation Buddhist orthodoxy may also suffer, for it may also be "reinterpreted" to fit local conditions and beliefs. But as the rural monkhood has become closely tied to the national Sangha, we might expect that rural monks have also become more sophisticated and more "orthodox" than in the past.

As far as we can tell, the indigenous Phu Thai religious system had neither a crystallized orthodoxy nor a core of codifiers and proselytizers dedicated to maintaining its belief intact. It is not surprising then that Buddhism has been able to permeate almost all of local religious belief. The villagers' identification with Buddhist universalism and a supra-local moral and institutional order may have played a significant role in breaking through the Phu Thai particularism in the realm of kinship and in paving the way for their inclusion in the national society.

Political Patterns in Nong Sung

If less dramatic than the changes in the sphere of village religion, the general changes that have taken place in the village political sphere are more clear-cut. The once integral and largely autonomous Phu Thai domain, headed by the Chao Mueang of Nong Sung, has been broken up into smaller units subordinate to and articulated with the national administration. In the past, the Chao Mueang seems to have actually possessed a measure of power which he could exert on the local scene, and contacts between Nong Sung and the Bangkok regime were few and largely restricted to the Phu Thai leadership. Today, local Phu Thai leaders have little, if any, real power, and the national government is represented by the centrally-appointed District Officer located only a short distance from the village. Political maneuvering within the old Phu Thai domain was linked to the indigenous system

of tutelary spirits and to manipulation of the local kinship and marriage system, and thus confined to local institutions and issues. Today, in Nong Sung at least, village tutelary spirits play an insignificant
role and national institutions and issues intrude themselves in village
politics.

Despite the proximity of the District Office and, in 1963, the personal popularity of the District Officer, from the perspective of most
Nong Sung villagers, there is a wide gap between the village sphere
and that represented by the national government.[9] This wide conceptual gap is manifested whenever a high ranking national or provincial
official happens to visit the village. On such occasions the official is
treated with exaggerated forms of deference and respect not dissimi-
lar to those accorded monks. Villagers willingly grant such officials
a status of almost qualitative superiority as they do to monks. But officials possess power that may be used arbitrarily and coercively, and
villagers are mistrustful of power or its potential use. Hence, unlike
their attitude toward monks, villagers' attitudes toward officials are often tinged with ambivalence. While the nearness of the District Office
makes such visits always imminent, they are not particularly frequent.

The national administration extends into the village through the
offices of the "*tambon* (commune) headman" (*kamnan*) and "village
(or hamlet) headman" (*phu yai ban*). Each of the two hamlets making
up Nong Sung has its own headman, and the headman of the western
hamlet also traditionally serves as the *tambon* headman as well. These
two local officers might be viewed as part of the national apparatus
because of their administrative duties, for which they receive small
salaries. However, from the perspective of the villagers (and of the
headmen themselves), these officers are a part of the local community, not "officials." They are expected to represent the village sphere
and to mediate between the village and the national government.
Most of the communication process that passes through the headmen
is one-way, from the top down. Local leaders have little leverage, and
small inclination, to exert pressure from the bottom up.

In contrast to the supra-village sphere represented by the national administration, the village sphere is seen as one in which status

---

[9] The District Officer was familiar with and sympathetic towards local customary practices,
local diet, and the local dialect. In addition to these factors, his father had been the
provincial official in charge of constructing the Nong Sung "airfield" many years ago. This
gave him especially close ties with the Phu Thai in general and Nong Sung in particular.

differences between individuals are not great. A formula which is a part of village rhetoric illustrates this view. On public occasions, the notion that villagers are "elder and younger siblings all together (*phi nong kan*) is frequently reiterated. This formula is not a claim of actual common descent or kinship between villagers, but rather asserts that the differences among villagers are of the same order as those between kinsmen. That is, the village is conceptualized as a body of "near equals" in status. However, within this framework of "near equality," hierarchical differences in status pervade almost every aspect of daily life and social interaction. These differences in status within the village are often phrased in kin terms in which age and sex distinctions are especially important.

There is no single objective factor which characterizes those individuals identified most frequently by informants as "village leaders." Most leaders are of mature age, in their forties, but some are considerably younger. There are also a few older village leaders in their fifties and sixties who have not yet retired from active life. Most leaders are prosperous by village standards, but a few are well below the median. There are also some very prosperous villagers who are not identified at all as leaders. Some leaders have extensive monastic experience or have a reputation for piety. Others have no monastic service or show little explicit concern with religion as such. The pattern of Nong Sung kinship is such that kinship affiliations play a secondary role in village leadership. Basically, village leadership is grounded in more subjective factors.

Leadership in village affairs is manifested by the ability to influence the activities of others and to mobilize their support. In general, ability to exert leadership in the village is a function of the "respect" (*khwamnapthue*) which an individual can engender among his fellow villagers. In the situation of "near equality" which is deemed to exist in the village, leadership is not simply a function of any office or position. The chief, but not the only, exception to this is the monkhood. Monks are automatically granted deference and respect by virtue of their status. As we saw, monks can mobilize the entire village on both ritual and non-ritual occasions. In this sense then, monks are village leaders. However, offices such as those of hamlet or *tambon* headman do not, by themselves, carry any great respect. A headman earns his office because of the respect others have for him. He does not have respect simply by virtue of his office. Hence, the two hamlet headmen in Nong Sung were not the sole, nor perhaps, the most effective leaders in the village.

Village leaders earn respect by manifesting personal qualities admired by other villagers. Leaders are characterized by informants as being especially knowledgeable or wise, although not necessarily well educated. Each leader is thought to manifest a modest and retiring demeanor, and yet to have a winning, almost seductive, personality. Leaders are also thought to be particularly well mannered and polite. By displaying such attributes, village leaders earn the approbation of their fellows, inducing them to seek out the leaders' advice and follow their directions. Leaders mobilize support by the force of their character or the charm of their personality. Thus, Nong Sung leaders do not impose any authority from above; they are "pushed up," as it were, by those who admire them, seek to emulate them, and are willing to follow them.

There is a broad agreement among informants about the kinds of qualities which deserve respect and few objective limits on leadership positions. This makes for an extremely complex political situation in village affairs. In theory at least, any villager may attempt to display the admired personal attributes and thus aspire to a local leadership position. In fact, of course, not every individual is capable of, or expert at, showing the appropriate qualities. Only a few men are held to be outstanding exemplars. Politically, the village is made up of a number of loosely defined and to some extent cross-cutting "factions" centering on such outstanding individuals.

There are several reasons why the membership and boundaries of village factions are difficult to discern. For one thing, leaders are not competing for positions of power but for positions of respect. Each leader manifests, in some degree, the *same* set of attributes or qualities which all other leaders display. In aligning himself with someone exemplary, a villager does not imply that other contenders for respect or leadership are characterized by an *absence* of the respect-earning qualities and are unworthy of respect. Factional alignments form because of differences in underlying subjective judgments about the relative *degree* of respect a particular leader deserves.

In the normal course of village life, membership in or affiliation with a particular leader's faction is revealed mainly by consistent patterns of interaction, while the boundaries of such groupings are marked by consistent patterns of avoidance. But the situation is actually more complex than this might suggest, for not all villagers are equally caught up in factional alignments, and there is considerable freedom for individual followers to shift their allegiance from one exemplary figure to another without difficulty or moral sanction. Thus, membership in factions may be unstable as a leader's ability to attract followers waxes or wanes *vis-à-vis* the ability of other contenders for leadership positions. Aside from this, villagers denigrate open conflicts or disputes between leaders or between followers. Hence, factional alignments rarely come into view.

Although the problem of village leadership is always imminent, some situations bring the problem into the open. One such occasion arose in 1960, before I began my investigation, involving the election of a new headman for the western hamlet of the village. Another situation in which village leadership came to the fore involved the extensive projects undertaken to improve the village temple in 1963. My efforts to reconstruct the election situation and observations of the temple projects indicated the main outlines of factionalism in Nong Sung. They also revealed that the national system has penetrated more deeply into the village than might be apparent at first. In particular, these situations illustrated that the villagers' ideology of "near equality" in the status of village members may be threatened by the intrusion of non-local factors in the village.

In 1963, the main lines of affiliation and cleavage in Nong Sung centered around two men: the incumbent headman of the western hamlet, who was also the *tambon* headman, and the village Schoolmaster, who was also the chief of the school teachers. There were also a number of "splinter factions" centering on other leading figures in the village, which were not firmly tied to the parties of the two leading contenders. Such splinter factions might boost their own leading figure against the other two, or perhaps swing their support behind one or the other.

Both the Headman and the Schoolmaster had been born and lived most of their lives in Nong Sung. Under most circumstances the rivalry for the leading position of respect within the village would focus largely on local interests and local issues and thus be confined to the personal characters of the contenders. In fact, the Headman's efforts to attract and mobilize followers was limited to manifesting the characteristics which other villagers admire. His position as headman did not assure him of any special following. The Schoolmaster also displayed the admired characteristics in his activities, but his position tended to introduce some non-local elements into village politics. In contrast to the Headman, the Schoolmaster's position gave him a coterie of supporters, in particular, the other village school teachers. Although these teachers seem to have admired the Schoolmaster as a person, they were aligned to him for reasons other than his character alone.

In 1963 there were fifteen teachers (including two women) living in Nong Sung. All the teachers were born and raised in the Northeast although nine were non-Phu Thai. Only eight teachers actually taught in the village school. The remaining seven teachers commuted from Nong Sung to the nearby villages where they taught. These commuting teachers preferred to live in the large village of Nong Sung which they thought more "convenient" and more "progressive" than the tiny remote villages in which they worked.

The common experiences and aspirations of teachers give them a degree of solidarity, as well as orientations which extend beyond the limits of the village and the region. Most of the local teachers are intensely interested in advancement within the framework of the Ministry of Education. Such promotion involves passing nationally-administered examinations. In particular, the younger teachers desire scholarships for advanced study, preferably in Bangkok or abroad. This is deemed the sure path to success, as demonstrated by one Nong Sung man who had actually received an M.A. from an American university and in 1963 had a good job in Bangkok. Thus, village teachers shared certain interests in common over and above the interests of ordinary villagers.

Aside from such common interests, teachers in general occupy a uniquely favored place in the village community. Their role as teacher benefits from positive attitudes toward "knowledge" derived from Buddhist beliefs. Teachers' salaries provide them with a stable economic base not available to most villagers, although many teachers augment their pay by engaging in part-time farming or trade. Their occupation involves teachers in a style of life which differs considerably from that of the ordinary villager, while their link with the national bureaucracy gives them an increment of the high status accorded "officials' without the ambivalence associated with positions of power. Hence, teachers have respect in the community by virtue of their positions. But these factors and their role as "cultural brokers" between the national culture and the local community orients them more than the ordinary villager to the larger national society.

The Schoolmaster shared these common interests and orientations with the other village teachers, while his position as their chief gave him a measure of authority over them. Thus, most, but not all, of the local teachers were aligned with the Schoolmaster. It is worth emphasizing that while the teachers did admire the personal qualities of the Schoolmaster, their affiliation with him was not geared simply to his character traits but was also influenced by his position and by the supra-local orientations they shared with him.

It is not surprising then that the Schoolmaster and his partisans tended to introduce national issues and national institutions into the local political scene. The 1960 election for headman of the western hamlet provides a good example. Because the Schoolmaster's position precluded him from running for this office, a member of his faction put himself forward as a candidate. The Schoolmaster's candidate was a vigorous man who identified himself as a farmer, but he had actually been a teacher for a time and was most famous in the village for his trading activities. As this man looked back on the election, he saw the contest revolving around an "issue," that of the "development" of the village and its locale. This issue is derived from the national government's current interest in the Northeast and is heavily propagandized by national officials. The eventual winner of the election took a "gradualist" stance on the issue and was purportedly supported by the older villagers, in particular, by the older women. The Schoolmaster's candidate, the eventual loser, proposed a program of "development now!" and claimed to have had the support of the young people and teachers. All the adult members of the western hamlet were eligible to vote in the election which was held in the temple yard and supervised by officials from the District Office. The election was won, or lost, by only twelve votes. In accounting for his loss, the Schoolmaster's candidate explained that although he had had the support of the village young people, some of them were too "shy" or "embarrassed" (*ay*) to publicly display their disagreement with elders.

An election for hamlet headman is clearly "political," but the contest between the Headman and the Schoolmaster for a position of leading respect in the community was not confined to such clear-cut situations. For example, although the projects aimed at improving the temple provided an opportunity for villagers to make merit and display their common Buddhist commitments, they also presented an opportunity for the Schoolmaster and the Headman to exhibit their respective qualities and strengths before the village. The Headman's ability to mobilize labor for these projects displayed his talents, while the Schoolmaster could offer more technical skills in drawing up plans. From the perspective of the Nong Sung political game, the excursion of the village children, led by the Schoolmaster to gather stones for the temple's foundation, was not only a meritful act but a shrewd symbolic blow at the Headman's strength. However, the Schoolmaster came into his own when it became clear that local resources could not complete the projects. He was then able to turn to his contacts in the national bureaucracy for assistance, a realm in which the Headman was no serious competitor.

In addition to their direct involvement in village factions, teachers have a more indirect but potent impact on the local political scene. Teachers introduce the national culture to the village children. They teach the national language, national values and ideologies, and national standards of etiquette and morality. The teachers serve as a bridge between the local community and the larger society, and the school has become an important focus of national political symbols. For example, at the school the national anthem is played and the national flag is hoisted each day while the students manifest respect for the King whose picture is displayed with an image of the Buddha on an altar in the school house.

The school system serves as an important channel for geographic and social mobility in Nong Sung. School teachers themselves are moved about, not always within their own districts. Thus nine of the teachers living in Nong Sung had come to live in the village from outside the district. In 1963 there were also twenty-three young people from Nong Sung studying full time outside the village. Their advanced education ranged from secondary school in nearby provincial towns to college and university level in Bangkok.

These young students' movement is more than simply geographic, for advanced education is geared to rising in the larger society. Insofar as they are successful, these students are pulled out of rural villages and into urban and national channels of mobility. Local teachers play a central role in the aspirations of village youth for advancement in the national society. Not only do they serve as a concrete model of such status advancement, but also provide education, the means for it. Apparently the local teachers' own ambitions for advancement are successfully communicated to the children they teach.

The changes that have taken place in Nong Sung's political sphere are complex. The national government successfully splintered the traditional Phu Thai domain and did away with the Chao Mueang system. This move tended to "equalize" the status of those living in the village sphere by removing local positions of power. Local political maneuvering no longer involved a competition for positions of power but for positions of respect within the local community. The criterion of leadership was reputation within the village and ability to mobilize support through force of character. The issues and resources involved in village leadership were largely if not exclusively local in nature. This situation was not markedly influenced by the extension of the national administration into the village through the offices of village and *tambon* (commune) headmen, for these officers are a part of the local community and share the interests and orientations of the mass of villagers.

The national educational system, through the medium of the village school and teachers, seems to have had greater impact on the local political scene than the formal administrative apparatus. Village teachers inculcate the national culture, national values, and national aspirations in village youth, thus promoting their inclusion in the larger society. In Nong Sung, the presence of a number of teachers living in the village has had direct effects on the local political scene by introducing national issues and national institutions into local political striving. Teachers' common style of life, common interests, and common orientations to the larger society have complexified the village status system. The position of teacher earns automatic respect, and the view of "near equality" in status among villagers is thereby threatened. As the training of local teachers becomes increasingly "professionalized" in regional and national teachers' colleges, such factors are likely to become more important in differentiating teachers from ordinary villagers.

Although the national government has played an important role in encouraging education in rural areas, in particular, by supplying teachers' training, paying salaries, and providing other forms of support through the Ministry of Education, if villagers were indifferent to education, these efforts would not have been as successful as they have been. In fact, Nong Sung villagers have been extremely responsive to education. For example, Nong Sung has had a "secular" school teacher at least since 1910, a very long time in Northeastern Thailand. The two large buildings housing the village school were also built and are maintained by local resources and initiative.

I should note that the active involvement of teachers in local politics and their supra-local orientation is not unique in Nong Sung. The Schoolmaster in neighboring Khamchai was also extremely active in village and local politics with unfortunate results. He and some of his supporters were arrested for "communist" activities.

The local school, supported by other factors, has had a paradoxical effect on the village. On the one hand, promoting inclusion in the national society has encouraged young people to leave the village and enter national channels of mobility. On the other hand, for those villagers who decide to remain within the rural village sphere, no matter what their reasons, Nong Sung has become a more attractive place to stay than the tiny remote villages in its environs. Nong Sung has taken on some of the attributes of the larger society and, in contrast to more isolated villages nearby, it is an exciting place where things happen.

Economic Activities in Nong Sung

When the Phu Thai migrated to Northeast Thailand, they sought out a particular type of environment for their settlements in the upland valleys paralleling the Mekong river. Their early economy was dominated by wet rice agriculture, supplemented by the production of a variety of vegetables, cotton, silk, and some hunting and fishing. Livestock production was also important in this early economy and Phu Thai men drove herds for sale to distant markets. Thus, this early Phu Thai economy was not exclusively a "subsistence" economy geared strictly to local requirements.

Changes in this basic economic system are less dramatic and clear-cut than those which have taken place in the village religious and political spheres. Some changes have taken place, and these may be related, in part, to more general changes in the economic situation of the Northeast as a region. For example, although livestock production is still important in the village economy, Phu Thai men no longer drive herds to urban markets. Such drives ceased, according to village informants, some 20-30 years ago. Today, traders from regional market centers such as Ubon come to Nong Sung and surrounding villages to buy livestock. This change can be related to the development of improved transportation facilities in the Northeast, in particular, the construction of railroad connections between the Northeast and the Central region.

Of course, Nong Sung is still situated in the upland ecological niche which early Phu Thai seem to have favored, whereas their Thai-Lao neighbors live in lower-lying valleys. These differing ecological situations have some implications for agriculture. The upland location of Nong Sung involves less danger from the disastrous floods which make production in the lowland areas extremely precarious. Conversely, the upland areas may be more affected by droughts or irregular rainfall. But the higher elevations are also more amenable to water control measures than are the lower elevations. The degree to which the people of Nong Sung have taken advantage of this possibility is striking, for the area is dotted with dams and other water control projects initiated by local leadership and carried out using local resources. It is also notable that the Schoolmaster of Nong Sung has been a leader in such undertakings.

The overwhelming majority of the villagers identify themselves as farmers, and more particularly, as rice farmers. Although households may cultivate fairly extensive gardens, only "rice land" (*na*) is counted by villagers. Such holdings are relatively small. The most common amount of rice land cultivated by a household is a plot of from six to ten *rai* (two and a half *rai* equals one acre), while the largest land holding reported by a villager is only fifty *rai*. A very small number of households have no access to rice land at all. Some teachers and a few elderly widows who still maintain separate households have no land, but only two viable village households have no land and hire out as farm laborers, raise livestock, or produce silk to eke out a living.

Unlike other areas in Thailand, there are not formal modes of obtaining cooperative labor in Nong Sung. Extra labor is commonly hired when needed either from within or outside the village. The small size of the village farms might have something to do with the absence of such cooperative forms of labor. However, any household farming fifteen to twenty *rai* or more can not cultivate without obtaining some additional help aside from the own household, at least for planting and harvesting.

The Phu Thai have a reputation among officials and their neighbors as industrious and hard-working. Official figures gathered by the Khamchai District Office support this reputation as well-founded. These figures permit a comparison between the Phu Thai communes (*tambons*) and the Thai-Lao communes that make up the District. On the average, the Phu Thai communes produce more buffalo, cattle, and pigs per household than do their Thai-Lao counterparts. Although the average number of *rai* planted to rice in Phu Thai communes is roughly the same as in the Thai-Lao communes, Phu Thai production of other agricultural crops is appreciably greater. For example, the Phu Thai communes plant 100 times as many *rai* to sesame as do the Thai-Lao communes. Comparative figures for other crops include: castor oil, sixteen times as many *rai* planted; maize, fifteen times as many *rai*; tobacco, seven times as many *rai*; kenaf, five times as many *rai*; cotton, three times as many *rai*; and sugar cane, twice as many *rai*. Moreover, ten times as many Phu Thai households produce silk as Thai-Lao households. There is some basis for the stereotype that the Phu Thai are industrious when compared to their neighbors.

The people of Nong Sung are more than hard-working; they are also deeply involved in a cash economy. Crops, such as sesame, castor oil, kenaf, and to some extent silk, are basically "cash" crops. The involvement of villagers with a cash economy is highlighted by the number of households which reported having sold some part of their production in the year prior to my investigation. Of the 232 households comprising the village, 104 reported having sold rice in 1962. Livestock sales were also common. For example, forty-eight households had sold one or more buffalo in 1962. Cattle had been sold by thirty-three households and pigs by ninety-four households. Production and sale of silk is another important feature of the village economy. Some seventy-nine households reported having sold some silk in 1962. The value of this silk, figured at village prices, amounted to about 52,000 baht (roughly $2,500).

Despite the relatively large size of the village, Nong Sung has no regular village market. Some petty marketing of vegetables, eggs, fish, and meat is carried out when the need or opportunity arises. This petty trade, as well as most aspects of gardening and silk production, is done largely by village women. Plow blades, hardware, dyes, kerosene lamps, tinned food, school supplies, and other goods are available in the several stores located in the village, or they may be obtained on trips to Mukdahan.

The Chinese merchant and store keeper is the only person involved in full-time trade in Nong Sung. He had come to Nong Sung some twenty-five years before from his birthplace in Ubon and was married to a Phu Thai girl from the neighboring village of Khamchai. Their children are of Phu Thai cultural status, although one daughter had married a hotel owner in Ubon (presumably a "Chinese"). Aside from maintaining the largest and best stocked store, the Chinese merchant operates a kerosene-run rice mill, located in a shed next to his store, and acts as a broker or agent for the sale of the various local products, such as rice, kenaf, and silk.

The Chinese merchant does not have a monopoly of village trade, for a number of villagers are also caught up in trading activities. However, the involvement of villagers in trade is largely part-time. There are eight part-time stores in Nong Sung, all less well-stocked than the store of the Chinese merchant, but overlapping in basic inventory with his store. Prices for the same goods are essentially the same in all the village stores, hence trade depends less on price competition than on factors such as convenience of location, terms of sale (e.g. credit), and matters of friendship or kinship. There are also three other kerosene operated rice mills owned and run by villagers aside from that owned by the Chinese merchant.

There are also a number of part-time specialties which supplement household income. For example, there are eight part-time tailors in the village. Tailoring is not an occupation for a poor person, for it involves a considerable outlay of money to purchase a machine and of time in learning to operate it. Tailoring also requires a good "credit standing," for cloth is purchased on credit either in Mukdahan or from cloth merchants (often Indians) who make occasional trips through the area. Most of the clothes these village tailors make are "western-style" trousers, shirts, and uniforms for teachers and local school children. Thus, these tailors reflect the penetration of modern ways into the community. Other part-time specialists in the village include: four wood workers or carpenters, four barbers, one tinsmith, and one bicycle repairman.

There are a number of village men who dominate the trade in local products, such as rice, silk, kenaf, and livestock. Generally these men act as brokers or agents for the sale of the local goods to urban markets. As in the case of the village stores, competition between local brokers is less in terms of price competition and more in terms of the conditions of sale or non-economic factors such as friendship. For example, all the village men who serve as middlemen for the sale of rice, including the Chinese storekeeper, are agents for the same Mukdahan rice mill. Thus, the prices they could offer were essentially the same. Price differentials and bargaining might occur with respect to "grading" the local produce (in particular of rice and silk), but even here bargaining was restricted by generally recognized limits with respect to acceptable price ranges. Aside from the brokers living in the village, the drivers of the busses that serve Nong Sung also act as middlemen. Occasionally, a non-local rice merchant may enter the village to buy directly from farmers.

There are a number of suggestive connections between the local educational institution and those most actively involved in village economic pursuits. For one thing, the two busses which serve Nong Sung are each owned by teachers, although neither owner actually lives in the village. One of the village rice mills is owned by a local teacher, while another teacher is very active as a broker in the livestock trade. The village Schoolmaster, who owns one of the largest farms in the village, is also a leader in initiating local water control projects. Other teachers, or members of their immediate families, are involved in part-time trade or other specialties, such as tailoring and woodworking.

The relationship between village economic activities and local educational institution is more subtle and pervasive than the direct contribution of teachers to economic activities, however potent that may be. For example, many of the leading traders and merchants in the village have some sort of close kinship or marriage tie with teachers, while the village school board included the Chinese merchant, another storekeeper, and a partner in one of the village rice mills.

The connection between these local entrepreneurs and school board membership is understandable. One of the chief duties of the school board is to maintain a benign interest in the school, in part, to supply financial support when it might be needed. Since traders are prosperous, and have cash, they are obviously ideal school board members.

The local political situation also influences the composition of the village school board. The Schoolmaster has a considerable voice in the appointment of school board members. Thus, the composition of the school board, in part, reflects the Schoolmaster's efforts to win the support of influential villagers. It should be noted, however, his efforts were not completely successful. Several leading merchants and members of the school board were, if not seeking leadership positions for themselves, allied to the Headman. Village traders also seek positions of leadership and respect in the community, a factor which further complicates Nong Sung's political scene.

There are other factors involved in the close link between traders and the village educational system. Both traders and teachers are engaged in activities which orient them toward the larger society more than the ordinary villagers. Local traders are, perhaps, less conscious of their involvement in the national economy than the teachers' awareness of their involvement with the national government and national culture. But both teachers and traders must be able to bridge the local and the supra-local realms. Traders use the national language, not the Phu Thai dialect, in their roles as brokers between the village and the urban economy. The facilities provided by the national government, such as improved roads, have an immediate impact and interest for traders. Traders must deal with fluctuations in the national, and world, economy. They must establish contacts in and be able to deal familiarly with regional and national urban situations. Thus, traders and teachers share some common orientations to the larger society which other villagers may not share to the same degree.

The relationship between economically oriented villagers, the educational institution, and the supra-local sphere goes beyond that observed for merchants and traders. It also includes leading farmers. For example, in the six households which owned the largest farms in the village (i.e. farms of 40-50 *rai*), there are a total of six teachers in the immediate family (although not all actually living in Nong Sung), one member of the village school board, three officials of the national government (also not living in the village), two female members married to non-local national officials, and five children away from the village getting some form of advanced education. The Schoolmaster is one of these prosperous land owners. We might speculate that common motivational and conceptual postures underlie these relationships between economic activities, education, and the larger social world into which Nong Sung villagers are being incorporated. However plausible such a speculation may be, we should not overlook potential areas of strain in this situation.

The man who lost the 1960 election for headman was allied with the Schoolmaster. He had once been a teacher himself before serving in the Thai army for a time. He had impeccable village kinship connections. He was a direct descendent of the family of the old Chao Mueangs, and his elderly father was especially respected as a pious man who was also the leading "soul-tying doctor" in the village. The candidate's wife was close kin to the headman of the eastern hamlet. Thus, he had numerous positive factors on his side. However, he was also, next to the Chinese merchant, the leading trader in the village. His personality fitted him well for that role, for he was vigorous, hearty, boisterous, and almost aggressive in his every action. These characteristics made him particularly successful in dealing with urban merchants. However, these are not the traits which earn respect in the village. According to informants who were aligned with the winner of the election, it was these traits that led him to lose the election, not the "embarrassment" of young people, as he himself saw it. Hence, there may be some incompatibility between the qualities that make for a good trader in the supra-local economy and the qualities that earn respect in the village. This could pose serious problems, and these problems still remain potential. Most traders still identify themselves primarily as farmers and are enmeshed more in the village sphere than in the national economy.

In summary, significant changes have taken place in the village economy. Nong Sung farmers are actively engaged in the production of goods for sale in urban markets. Local merchants and traders mediate between village farmers and the national economy. The contributions of the national government to this altered economic situation seem to have been more indirect than direct. The government has provided an economic infra-structure by construction of public works and a suitable climate for economic activities. But the participation of villagers in this cash economy has stemmed largely from individual and local initiatives.

Village merchants and traders have a vested interest in a stable marketing situation and improved transportation facilities. These factors lead them to bring supra-local issues into the village scene. Merchants, traders, and prosperous farmers, as well as teachers, share certain common orientations to the supra-village sphere. Although these local entrepreneurs do not, by any means, form a solidary group within the village, their presence and identification with the larger society adds a further dimension of complexity to the local status system.

The impact of traders on the village is less clear-cut than that of teachers. They have, perhaps, made living in Nong Sung more attractive to ordinary villagers by encouraging the prosperity of the area. More subtly, they may have made the village a more inviting place to live simply because it is a more complex and exciting place than the tiny and more remote villages nearby. It seems clear that desire for advancement in the national economic sphere, as such, is less potent than desire for advancement within the Sangha or the bureaucracy. However, the increased prosperity which the traders directly encourage in the village may provide the means for more village youth to aspire for these other forms of advancement away from the village. Hence, it is largely, but not exclusively, the children of prosperous village leaders who leave the village to acquire advanced education and to enter national channels of mobility.

Discussion

The evidence from Nong Sung indicates that the Phu Thai of this area have changed from an isolated ethnic enclave and are becoming a part of the larger and more inclusive social world. The people of Nong Sung have simultaneously become increasingly "Buddha-ized" and "Thai-icized." Monks, teachers, and traders, each in their own way, serve as bridges between the village and the larger society. On the one hand, these men, in varying degrees, introduce supra-local and national elements into the village scene. On the other hand, they provide channels from the village into the larger society. Patterns of village social life have been modified through their influence.

Buddhist symbols, values, and beliefs now permeate village religion, thereby undermining the particularistic and localized indigenous religion in which beliefs about ancestral spirits and village tutelary spirits were prominent. The erosion of beliefs about ancestral spirits has had implications for marriage practices, residence patterns, and inheritance. The relationship between husband and wife is now the central issue in marriage rituals, not the tie between a woman and her parents. Young nuclear families are free to locate where they may maximize their own position without the intrusion of beliefs about ancestral spirits which once limited their freedom. The freedom of young couples to locate and affiliate where they wish has, in turn, had some impact on inheritance patterns, which once gave women special rights to their parents' houses.

Identification with a universal Buddhist moral order has seduced villagers away from a heavy dependence on a system of localized tutelary spirits. The Buddhist moral order both includes and transcends the village. The village temple and monks bring the abstract Buddhist order directly into the village itself. Monks are proximate symbols of Buddhist values. They serve as the focus of ritual activities in which villagers reveal their commitment to those values and their identification with a diffuse, loosely defined Buddhist moral community. The Sangha is itself a potent religious symbol, and its national organization provides the institutional framework that gives the Buddhist moral community its shape. The commitment and identification of villagers with this superordinate institutional and symbolic order encourages their inclusion in a society that extends beyond the confines of village and locality. Indeed, achievement and mobility within this superordinate order is an explicit value held by villagers.

Buddhism is the state religion of Thailand and the national Department of Religious Affairs looks after the interest of the Sangha. Thus, the national society is also a part of the Buddhist moral community. But national values and the national culture enter Nong Sung most clearly through the medium of the village school and local teachers. Aside from directly imparting the national culture in their teaching, teachers communicate to village youth their own orientations toward the larger society and their own aspirations for advancement within the national system. Village teachers are not only nearest models for advancement and inclusion in the nation, but also provide both the motives and the means to achieve these goals.

The presence of a large number of teachers living in Nong Sung has had some impact on the village status system and the local political situation. Teachers are granted an automatic increment of respect because of their position, whereas the ordinary villagers must earn respect through their character and activities. In Nong Sung, teachers form a relatively well-defined group with common interests and orientations to the larger society which differ, in some degree, from those of the mass of the villagers. Teachers have not only tended to introduce national issues and institutions into village politics, but their respected position has itself contributed an extra dimension of complexity to the village status system.

Improved transportation facilities have linked regional and national markets, providing increased economic opportunities in Northeast Thailand. The people of Nong Sung have responded to these opportunities. Village farmers have diversified and intensified their production, while a vigorous group of local traders and merchants mediate between the village producers and the urban markets where their goods are sold. The impact of the increased economic activity and the linkage between the village and urban economy is less clear-cut than the changes that have taken place in other spheres of village life.

Village brokers and prosperous farmers do not form a solidary group as do teachers. But those villagers who are most caught up in modern economic activities, like teachers, are oriented more to the larger society than are most villagers. Such men also encourage the intrusion of national issues into local politics and may form coalitions with others who share their supra-local interests. Despite their lack of solidarity as a group, brokers and prosperous farmers have helped to increase the complexity of village politics and leadership. In addition, increased economic activity has contributed to Nong Sung's relative prosperity, offering the economic means for village youth to seek advancement in the national society.

The deep penetration of Buddhism within village religion justifies the assertion that the people of Nong Sung have become increasingly "Buddha-ized." The proposition that they have also become increasingly "Thai-icized" may need some clarification.

Basically there has been a shift in "identity" in what "being Phu

Thai" means. It appears that formally being Phu Thai was seen in opposition to being a member of any other ethnic cultural category. Today, being Phu Thai is seen as a special variant within the larger framework of the Thai nation. Thus, when Phu Thai seek inclusion in the larger society, they do not have to repudiate their Phu Thai-ness. Nor does identification as a Phu Thai carry any negative connotations in the national society, as does identification as a "Thai-Lao" or "Northeasterner." Hence, large numbers of Phu Thai living in Bangkok have recently formed a "Phu Thai Association" which brings them together for social purposes.

It should also be noted that the Thai culture entering Nong Sung is the national culture emanating from Bangkok. Thus, in becoming "Thai-icized," Nong Sung is not becoming more like the farming villages of the Central region. It is becoming more like a Thai town or city. Many young villagers have a vision of a future Nong Sung which they express in idle talk and fantasy. This vision is of paved streets and automobiles, of electricity and television, of movie houses, stores, and markets. That is, they envisage the Nong Sung of the future with urban trappings.

It would be premature to see the increasing complexity in the village status system as the development of "classes" of officials and traders. But in some measure, the status system of Nong Sung is becoming more like that of an urban center rather than like the community of "near equals" typical of most farming villages. Perhaps this complexity in the village status system increases its appeal as a place to live.

The changes that have occurred in Nong Sung have not all come about smoothly. Numerous ambiguities and strains have accompanied them. For some villagers, surprisingly few, there is nostalgia for the kind of society which they conceive existed in the days of the old Chao Mueangs. For others, there is a longing for the simple undifferentiated village life that existed in the recent past. There is ambivalence even among those most oriented to the larger society. In particular, young men may be resentful about barriers to their inclusion in the larger society or about the speed of that inclusion. This resentment may be manifested in rowdyism on the local scene or projected onto the larger society. It may be no accident of ecological situation that areas of "insurgency" in the Northeast are also areas where Phu Thai are concentrated.[10]

Nong Sung has had an unusual history. It is larger than most villages and serves as a *tambon* (commune) center for other villages in its vicinity. It has changed to a greater degree than many, if not most, villages in Northeast Thailand. But every village, even the "typical" village, is unique. Although the processes which have influenced Nong Sung are clearly conditioned by special local factors, they are not unique. These processes are general throughout Northeast Thailand and the rest of the nation. Perhaps the special characteristics of Nong Sung may provide insights into the operation of those general processes in other villages where their impact is less apparent. If nothing else, Nong Sung illustrates that it is difficult to understand any village in Northeast Thailand today without taking into account the larger society in which it is placed and into which it is moving.

---

[10] See Peter Braestrup, "How the Guerrillas Came to Koh Noi" in *The New York Times Magazine*, December 10, 1967, especially the map on p. 49. Compare this map showing areas of "insurgency" in the Northeast with Map One above showing concentrations of Phu Thai.

Road to Nong Sung during the rainy season (1963)

Tilling a rice field for planting in Nong Sung (1963)

Planting rice in Nong Sung (1963)

Rice harvesting time in Nong Sung (1963)

Silk worms and cocoons in Nong Sung (1963)

A Family loom under a house in Nong Sung (1963)

**The entire community gathering for the Kathin ceremony
in Nong Sung (1963)**

The urban family in front of their house in a Bangkok suburb (1992)

A visit to Nong Sung by Charles and Jane Keyes (1963)

from left to right

back row: Charles Keyes, Schoolmaster, Tom Kirsch

middle row: Schoolmaster's eldest daughter, Jane Keyes, Schoolmaster's wife

front row: Schoolmaster's sixth daughter, elder son, seventh daughter, younger son, and fifth daughter

A Tale of Two Thai Families

Reflections on Social Change

Yohko Tsuji

Introduction

When he lived in Thailand in 1962-64, my husband, A. Thomas Kirsch, was "adopted" by two families. One was an urban Thai family in Bangkok. Tom became a part of this family through their youngest son, Lek, whom he met shortly after his arrival in Thailand. Lek's family provided Tom with a Bangkok home where he stayed for several months before moving to upcountry to conduct research and during his occasional breaks from the stern village life. The other was the Schoolmaster's family in Nong Sung, a remote Phu Thai village in Northeast Thailand. Tom lived with this family for an entire year and carried out his dissertation research in the village.

These two families were also the foci of my husband's last research in Thailand in 1992. As a Fulbright researcher, he spent six months from February to August in Bangkok. In his research proposal, he stated that his aim was "to gauge the qualitative and human effects of the profound changes that have occurred in Thailand over the last three decades on the families and their members."[1]

He did not have the opportunity to write up his data, however. The persistent sore throat, which he had attributed to Bangkok's polluted air, was diagnosed as cancer when he returned home. He had a laryngectomy in October 1992, and his long battle against recurring cancer continued for over six and a half years until his death in May 1999.

When the plan to publish a collection of Tom's works came up after his death, his colleagues asked me to contribute this essay because, accompanying Tom to Thailand twice, I came to know his Thai families well. Unfortunately, the publication project did not materialize. Because years have passed since I wrote this paper in 2000, I have added an epilogue to update the lives of his two Thai families, whom I visited in Thailand in 2007.

---

[1] A. Thomas Kirsch. 1991. "A Social History of Two Thai Families: 1960-1990." A research proposal submitted to the Fulbright Research Committee.

Tom greatly valued the friendship of these two families and fondly remembered his life with them. His experiences in Nong Sung became a lasting intellectual influence until the end of his days. In this essay, I shall introduce the reader to my husband's Thai families to whom he owed so much. Like Tom, I am a cultural anthropologist and have participated in many field trips with him and/or other researchers in Thailand. However, I am not a Thai specialist and have conducted no long-term, systematic study of the Kingdom. Therefore, I am in no position to offer the kind of social history of the two Thai families that Tom would have written had he not fallen ill. Instead, my article outlines some major changes that have occurred to them in the last four decades, based on what Tom wrote and said about their lives in the early 1960s and on what I heard and observed on my three trips to Thailand: two with Tom in 1985-86 and 1992 and one in 2000 after his death.

My Relationship with Tom's Two Families in Thailand

I met both families in 1985 when Tom and I went to Thailand together. He was on sabbatical leave from Cornell and served as Fulbright Consultant for a full academic year at Khon Kaen University in Northeast Thailand. This was my first trip to Thailand, and it required a lot of adjustments. My initial difficulties were intensified because we lived in a provincial town and I did not speak Thai. I also found Thai culture fundamentally different from any other I had lived in. As a result, I experienced many frustrations and much confusion until I began to see the "native's logic" and learned enough Thai to get around.

In addition to the cultural problems, I had another difficulty: lost identity. Tom and I had been married for just one year. Back in America, I retained my own identity apart from being his wife. I also had my own circle of friends. No one thought of me simply as Tom's wife. In Thailand, however, I was an accompanying spouse without an independent identity. Neither of us had anticipated this problem, though as anthropologists, we had been prepared, at least intellectually, for my initial culture shock.

Tom's Thai families helped me cope with this personal dilemma by "adopting" me as they had Tom more than two decades earlier. On my first visit to Nong Sung in October 1985 for *Awk Phansa* (the festival to mark the end of the rainy season), we stayed in the Schoolmaster's house together with his children and grandchildren who returned home on this festive occasion. The family extended me such a warm welcome that hearing the children addressing their parents, I began to call the Schoolmaster and his wife "Khun Pho" (Father) and "Khun Mae" (Mother). Apparently, these sentiments were mutual. In January 2000 when I saw the Schoolmaster, he told me that Tom was his eldest son and I was his eldest daughter-in-law.

During the same trip, Lek, the youngest son of Tom's urban Thai family, shared with me a surprisingly similar remark by his late mother. Reminiscing about the early 1960s when Tom was staying with his family, Lek mentioned, "My mother always said Tom was one of her sons." If she had been alive when I met her son's family in 1985, I believe that she would have treated me as her daughter-in-law. By the time I met Lek, his mother had been dead for quite some time, and his nuclear unit—wife, son, and himself—had moved to a suburban home away from the family's ancestral home in central Bangkok. Nevertheless, Tom and I became a part of Lek's extended family, and his teenage son called us Uncle and Aunt.

Being a part of Thai families—having two people whom I could call Mother and Father and having a "nephew" who called me Aunt— gave me a sense of belongingness in an unfamiliar land. The fact that I was connected to these people only through my marriage to Tom did not diminish the comfort of finding a social niche I could fit into.

Though our visits to Thailand were not frequent for the last fifteen years, we had kept in touch with our two Thai families. Needless to say, we always saw them when we returned to Thailand. This did not change after Tom's death. I saw both families on my trip in early 2000.[2] It was very consoling to share my sorrow with them as well as memories of Tom. Hearing them reminisce about Tom's earlier years in Thailand also lifted my spirits. In addition, the village family played a very important role in helping me accomplish the major aim of my trip: to place Tom's ashes in Wat (temple) Triphun in Nong Sung.

---

[2] As mentioned in the Epilogue, I went to Thailand again in 2007 and reunited with our two Thai families.

The Urban Family[3]

My husband's urban family had six sons and two daughters. In 1962, when he met their youngest son, Lek, they lived in a "very large Western style two-story house of brick and stucco located on a narrow lane just off one of Bangkok's major roads."[4] Though Lek's father and eldest brother had died a few years earlier, his mother, a matriarch, kept the family together under the same roof. It was an extended family in the true sense of the term, including married children and their families as well as other kin who made their home there or stayed in the house for varying periods.[5]

Government service was the family tradition, though some of the children were engaged in other occupations.[6] They claim that this tradition dated back to as early as the Ayutthayan period (1569-1767). Lek's late father had been a senior official in the Treasury Ministry. Lek deviated from this pattern and was working as headwaiter at a German restaurant in Bangkok when Tom met him in 1962. But this was a temporary arrangement during a transitional period. He had just returned from Germany where he had received engineering training and wanted to maintain his proficiency in the language. Eventually, he, too, followed the family tradition and worked as an engineer for the Rural Electrification Authority, a government department.

In 1978, when Tom made a brief visit to Thailand, he met the Sino-Thai woman Lek had married and their six-year-old son. He also found that Lek's mother was still going strong, and the old family home in central Bangkok continued to be busy with people and their activities.

---

[3] Since I know only the youngest son, Lek, and his nuclear unit, the account of this family is much shorter than that of the village Schoolmaster's.

[4] Kirsch 1991.

[5] Tom had a totally unexpected reunion with one of Lek's nieces when the King's private secretary visited Cornell in the mid-1980s. At the reception held in his honor, his wife introduced herself as Lek's niece. Since she was a child when Tom was staying with the family, he could not recognize the young woman. She, however, identified him as her uncle's *farang* or Western friend.

[6] For instance, the eldest son, who died young, was an architect of great promise, and another son once worked as a manufacturer's agent for an international equipment company. One of the daughters owned a small dress shop.

This picture had changed so drastically when Tom returned to Thailand seven years later that he wrote: "In 1985-86, this previously lively household had, for practical purposes, broken up."[7] The house was occupied only by one son, his family, and one unmarried daughter. All the other children had moved elsewhere. Lek's nuclear family was living in a housing development near the Bangkok airport. In the mid-1980s, this northern suburb of the capital still retained a lot of greenery, allowing its residents a little taste of country life.

My husband saw two major factors behind the dispersal of his urban Thai family. The first was the impact of social change on the individual's life. Lek's family told him that Bangkok's traffic jam made daily commuting "prohibitively time-consuming"[8] and relocation highly desirable. Secondly, the death of the matriarch, Lek's mother, further precipitated the breakup of the once large household.

Moving to the northern outskirts of Bangkok brought Lek closer to his work place. But his son traveled two hours each way to attend a private school in the heart of Bangkok. In their view, the prestige of the school and the quality of education it offered justified this four-hour daily commute.

By 1992, when Tom made his last trip to Thailand, the investment in good education had already born fruit. Lek's son was studying physics at Chulalongkorn University, a school that has very high admission standards and is accorded the highest prestige and authority in the nation. Though this meant four more years of time-consuming daily trips to the center of Bangkok, a degree from Chulalongkorn promised a future among the elite in Thai society. Like his father, Lek's son also planned to study in the West for a graduate degree to advance his status further.

---

[7] Kirsch 1991.

[8] Kirsch 1991.

In 1992, Tom noticed a major change in Lek's life: his retirement from government service. He also observed that Thailand had changed tremendously even in the six years since his previous visit.[9] The waves of change did not miss the area where Lek's family lived. Bangkok's urban sprawl completely swallowed the once idyllic outskirts, replacing paddy fields and open lands with expensive, Western-style housing estates. Renovation also transformed Lek's house, a two-storied, dark-brown wooden structure, into a fashionable, Western-style home with a balcony whose white stucco shone under the tropical sun.

Westernization penetrated the family's shopping habits as well. A number of massive supermarkets opened near their home, selling groceries and other daily necessities in bulk at discount prices. Like their counterparts in the United States, these stores are designed to serve customers who own automobiles. Since his wife did not drive, Lek, now retired, went shopping with her once a week.

Though Tom's illness prevented him from returning to Thailand after 1992, he learned through correspondence that Lek's son's career plan was progressing smoothly. He graduated from Chulalongkorn University with a B.S. in 1993 and received an M. S. in 1995. In 1996, after teaching at his alma mater for one year, he was awarded a government scholarship to study in Sweden for a Ph.D. in physics. By mandating ten-year teaching service in Thailand after finishing the degree, this scholarship virtually guaranteed a faculty position at Chulalongkorn University for Lek's son.

The scholarship also expanded his horizon far beyond the boundaries of his own country. Since moving to Sweden, for instance, Lek's son had visited America three times to attend conferences, though his tight schedule allowed him to visit us in Ithaca only by phone. His parents' lives also came to include a broader world. Lek and his wife had visited their son in Sweden and planned another trip in summer 2000. They also maintained close contact with their son via e-mail.

----

[9] For instance, beside fancy shopping malls, high-rise condominiums, and luxurious housing estates, American fast food stores mushroomed everywhere, becoming a part of Thai middle-class life. Near our apartment on the Thonburi side of Bangkok (across the Chao Phraya River from the city center), Pizza Hut, Dunkin Donut, and McDonald's had opened and filled with Thai customers. This was a drastic change from 1985-86 when there was only one McDonald's in the entire nation and Dunkin Donut and Pizza Hut were unheard of. This first McDonald's was located just around the corner from the Erawan Hotel in the heart of Bangkok and catered mainly to foreign tourists and residents.

In early 2000, I saw all three members of Tom's urban Thai family in Bangkok. Lek's son came home during his winter break. With only a few years left to finish his Ph.D., he began to search for an institution in Western Europe where he could receive his post-doctoral training before settling down in his homeland. Lek's son's academic career is different from his father's engineering career in the electrification of Thailand's rural areas. Nonetheless, the son follows in the steps of his forebears; he chooses government service by teaching at the nation's most respected university.

While Lek's son has a definite career plan, his private life contains more unknowns. For instance, there are as yet no prospects for marriage even though he is a well-qualified bachelor in his late twenties. When Lek's son eventually marries, where will he and his wife make their home? Will they stay with his parents or with hers? Or, will they prefer to live neolocally? If the last is their choice, will they move back with their parents when the latter are old and widowed?

These questions will be answered only with the passage of time. What is certain is that Lek's son's life is enacted on a much larger stage than that of his parents, one that includes Thailand as well as the world beyond.

The Village Family

Nong Sung in the Early 1960s

In 1963, my husband lived with the village Schoolmaster's family while conducting his dissertation research. He described the remoteness of the village and its isolation at the time:

> The Northeastern village I lived in through most of 1963 was a bit beyond the "end of the road." In the rainy season, it was inaccessible to motor vehicles for extended periods. No matter what mode of travel was used, it took at least two days to reach the village from Bangkok.[10]

Why did Tom choose such an out-of-the-way place to study? From the beginning, he eyed Northeast Thailand as his field site because not much research had been done on this largest and poorest region of Thailand. During his pre-fieldwork exploration of the area, he hap-

---

[10] Kirsch 1991.

pened to come across Nong Sung and was captured by its idyllic beauty. A pond lay peacefully immediately behind the village and beyond it were green, gently-sloping hills. Without any hesitation, he told me many years later, he made up his mind to choose Nong Sung as his village[11] and returned to Bangkok to take care of various bureaucratic requirements for conducting research.

Several months later, Tom was back in Nong Sung again after a long, difficult journey from the capital by bus and buffalo cart. What awaited him was a completely new universe. A Harvard graduate student on his first field trip, he found many unaccustomed things: the language and culture as well as the tropical climate, the rice-centered diet, and the agrarian life style. These basic aspects of human life were not only highly different from his own in America, but they were not even similar to those in central Thailand where he had stayed for months prior to his move to the village.

For example, villagers in Nong Sung grew and ate a different variety of rice from what Thais in the central region favored. While *khaw jaw*, long-grain rice, was the staple for the latter, the former, like their Thai-Lao neighbors, ate *khaw niaw*, short-grain sticky rice, using their fingers.

Their languages were different. Even though people in Nong Sung were able to speak Thai, the national language, they used Phu Thai, a local tongue, for their daily communication. Thus, learning Phu Thai became an indispensable task for Tom. The Schoolmaster's eldest daughter recalled that Tom asked her and others to translate Phu Thai words into Thai and made his own dictionary with three columns, one each for Thai, Phu Thai, and English. In his letters from Nong Sung in the early stage of his field work, Tom often remarked on his discouragement and concern about being unable to learn the local language quickly enough.[12]

Living in the village in 1963 was like slipping backward in a time tunnel. There was no electricity or running water in village homes.

---

[11] The fact that Nong Sung was a Phu Thai village also encouraged Tom to make this quick decision. He was interested in studying minority groups living in the hills close to the national border in the North but had to give up this idea due to sensitive political situations there.

[12] I am grateful for Charles Keyes who brought to us a copy of the letters Tom had sent to him from Nong Sung when Cornell held a symposium in my husband's honor in February 1999.

Drinking water was acquired during the rainy season by channeling rain water into big clay jars and was used throughout the year. The diet mainly consisted of what people produced or caught themselves: rice, vegetables, and occasional meat and fish. It lacked variety as well as a balance of nutrients. Since farming, the livelihood of most villagers, depended on precarious rainfall, the procurement of food and decent drinking water was not always assured. A doctor who visited Nong Sung with his government's development team during Tom's research said that the lack of balanced diet and decent drinking water was a major cause of various health problems in the region.[13]

The isolation of the village also curtailed access to consumer goods, such as cigarettes, alcohol, and films. Tom was shocked to learn that the nearest place where he could buy Mekong, Thai whisky, was twenty kilometers from Nong Sung. Not a part of the local diet, bread, too, disappeared from his life. But once in a great while, he enjoyed the luxury of eating good French bread, which some villagers fetched for him in Laos, crossing the Mekong River from Mukdahan, a city on its bank thirty-five kilometers from Nong Sung.

Owing to its remoteness, communication with the rest of the world was not easy, either. The government postal service had yet to reach Nong Sung. Therefore, once a week, *kamnan* or the *tambon* (commune) head, picked up mail for the entire village at the post office in Khamchai, the *Amphoe* (District) Center six kilometers away. For out-going mail, anyone visiting the *Amphoe* Center served as Tom's courier. When his mother passed away in March 1963, his brother's cable from America was garbled and mostly incomprehensible.[14] Though it at least informed Tom of his mother's death, he had to make the long journey to Bangkok to make an international call for more details.

Nong Sung in 1963 had neither television nor movie theaters, making its evening rather dull. What little entertainment existed then was sporadic and often provided by visitors from the outside world. For instance, the Army Mobile Development Team and the traveling medicine salesman showed movies in the village. Drawing huge

---

[13] A. Thomas Kirsch. 1963 (July 15). A letter from Nong Sung to Charles Keyes.

[14] One of the reasons for this problem was that the cable was translated into Thai in Bangkok and forwarded to the post office in Mukdahan where the machine could not decode English.

crowds, these movies proved to be a good public relations device and helped their sponsors accomplish their educational or commercial missions. Tom also sponsored some entertainment. In October 1963, for example, he "...treated the village to a 'shadow play' to celebrate the victory of *Tambon* in a sports rally against two other *tambons*".[15]

Life in Nong Sung during my husband's first fieldwork was austere from an American point of view. It lacked the material abundance and comfort which most Americans took for granted. Absence of privacy also made village life difficult for Westerners.

Bathing in cold water aptly symbolizes these two aspects of village life four decades ago. Contrary to our assumptions, the weather in the tropics may be cool at certain times of the year. In Nong Sung, which is located in higher elevation than the Central Plain, temperature drops to as low as the forties or even to the thirties. Imagine lacking hot water in those "winter" months! It was tempting, of course, to skip daily bathing. But wrote Tom, "...there have been several cool-cool days when I could have forgone the doubtful pleasures of even that one bath a day—but such things are too public here to skip without causing comment".[16] Tom also told me a story which made him realize that villagers did not have the concept of privacy. One day, noticing Tom's pensive mood, a young man asked him what was the matter with him. Hearing Tom answering that he missed being alone once in a while, this man said, "Let's go somewhere where we can be alone together."

The unfamiliar climate and material deprivation, especially the low-protein intake, precipitated a grave health problem for Tom.[17] He

---

[15] A. Thomas Kirsch. 1963 (October 15). A letter from Nong Sung to Charles Keyes. Nong Sung was the *tambon* (commune) headquarters then. See Kirsch in this volume for the government administrative structure of the region.

[16] In this letter to Charles Keyes dated February 22, 1963, Tom mentioned his discovery that villagers in Nong Sung took one bath a day, normally before evening meal, compared with the three-baths-a-day routine in the village William Klausner studied.

[17] His meals contained twice as much protein as those of the villagers. On this special treatment, Tom wrote in his letter, "...the *Nai Amphoe* [District Head] has been giving instructions (orders?) concerning what *farangs* [Westerns] expect or need. As a result, I am treated considerably more like a guest than I would like. For example, instead of the regular diet of the village, I have a special menu prepared for me, consisting mostly of Bangkok style food—supervised by the daughter of my host, who graduated from a school of home economics in Bangkok. I undoubtedly get about twice as much protein in my daily diet than anyone else in the village—though I must confess the food is really good" (A. Thomas Kirsch. February 1, 1963. A Letter from Nong Sung to Charles Keyes).

contracted tropical sprue, a disease resulting in serious malfunctioning of the digestive organs and alarming weight loss. Though what induces tropical sprue is unknown, genetic predisposition makes some people susceptible to it when exposed to a drastic change of climate and diet. Unfortunately, Tom was among them. This was one major reason why he did not return to Nong Sung until 1978.

Village Family in the Early 1960s

Tom's host, the Schoolmaster, was also a farmer with a large land holding. He lived with his family in a big house, one of only two two-storied houses in the village in 1963. He and his wife had eleven children, of whom two had died in infancy. Of the nine surviving children, seven daughters and two sons, only five were home during Tom's residence in their household.

The eldest daughter (D1), having finished her higher education in Bangkok, was teaching at the village elementary school administered by her father. Others—two daughters (D6 and D7) and two sons (S1 and S2)—were the youngest four of the family. D6 commuted daily to a nearby village in order to enroll in school beyond the four years available in the village school. The two sons were pupils of the village school. D7 was a pre-schooler.

Four other daughters (D2, D3, D4, and D5) had left home either for work or for education. The second daughter (D2), a civil servant in Bangkok, had won a government scholarship and was studying sericulture in Japan. The third (D3) and the fourth (D4) lived in the central region, receiving nurse's and technical training respectively. The fifth daughter (D5) lived in Mukdahan, thirty-five kilometers from the village, where she attended high school.

Though Nong Sung in the early 1960s was "a bit beyond the 'end of the road',"[18] the influence of the outside world had already penetrated into the Schoolmaster's family and taken some members away from home. Tom remarked, "Although the everyday lives of those living in the household were deeply embedded in the village's agrarian life style, it is also clear that they were already taking advantage of the emerging new opportunities and changed conditions at the national

---

[18] Kirsch 1991.

level."[19] Advanced education, as he noted, provided an important channel, not only for geographic mobility, but for "rising in the larger society."[20]

Nong Sung and the Village Family in 1985-1986 [21]

The expansion of Tom's village family into the broader outside world continued steadily and, as will be shown below, successfully for the next two decades. In 1985, Tom returned to Thailand to serve as Fulbright Consultant at Khon Kaen University. For ten months, we lived in Khon Kaen, a provincial town in the center of Northeast Thailand. During this period, we had numerous opportunities, including two trips to Nong Sung, to see his village family and learn about the many changes that had occurred in their lives since 1964.

On "the extraordinary changes" he observed in 1985-1986, Tom made the following comment several years before his death:

> In the 1980s what had 20 years before been a Phu Thai village's "public arena" had been transformed into a "private lawn." This transformation not only marks a transition in the status of a single village family but reflects the extent to which the once clear boundary between "rural" and "urban" Thailand has been muted if not completely abrogated.[22]

There were many other changes in the village and surrounding area. For instance, increasing development in Northeast Thailand resulted in a major reorganization in the government administrative structure. In 1982, the Province of Mukdahan was created by dividing Nakhon Phanom Province. In 1985 Nong Sung was upgraded to a *king amphoe* (sub- district) headquarters of this new province.

Another noteworthy change was much easier access to Nong Sung by an all-weather road constructed in the 1970s. In October 1985, we took a bus from Khon Kaen to the village. The four-hour ride through the idyllic countryside was a comfortable one on a paved, two-lane

---

[19] Kirsch 1991.

[20] Kirsch in this volume, p. 46.

[21] In 1978, during his brief stay in Thailand, Tom went to Nong Sung to see his village family. However, he left too few records for me to write about this revisit.

[22] A. Thomas Kirsch. Undated (circa 1998) Unfinished Manuscript.

highway all the way to the Nong Sung bus stop.[23] A dirt road extended from the bus stop to the center of the village, a distance of ten minutes on foot. We were spared this walk, however. To our surprise, a young village entrepreneur was waiting at the bus stop to transport passengers in his colorfully-painted *tuk tuk*, the three wheeled minitruck seen in cities. Conspicuously written on its side was its name, Sky Lab, in English.

By 1985, Nong Sung had long been electrified. Young children cleaning the kerosene lamps with their tiny hands, a sight familiar to Tom during his initial stay, belonged to the past. At the Schoolmaster's house, an electric pump brought running water, and several electric fans made the hot weather more tolerable. There was also a washing machine outside the bathroom, formerly open but now enclosed.[24] Modernization in the kitchen appeared in the form of a propane gas stove and oven. We were surprised to see the oven at the Schoolmaster's house, because our house in Khon Kaen did not have one, even though it was a Western-style house originally built for scholars from New Zealand. In addition to these modern conveniences in the Schoolmaster's home, we saw many consumer goods in the village stores. We bought a roll of film in Nong Sung. Bread, too, was regularly stocked at the village stores. There was no longer a need to cross the Mekong to Laos to obtain French bread.[25]

The Schoolmaster's family had changed as much as Nong Sung. By October 1985, when Tom and I visited Nong Sung, none of his children lived at home. Though his big two-storied house looked the same as before, it had only four residents: the Schoolmaster, his wife, and two young relatives from a nearby village. These young people performed various chores while attending the village school, now expanded to include six years of schooling and some technical education.

---

[23] Since daily flights connected Khon Kaen and Bangkok in one hour, it was possible to leave the capital in the morning and reach Nong Sung by early afternoon. The same distance could also be traveled within ten hours by car.

[24] Before our departure to Nong Sung, one of our neighbors, a professor at Khon Kaen University who had a Ph.D. from Cornell, gave me *pha thung*, a cloth Thai women wrap their body when bathing in public. Since the bathroom at the Schoolmaster's house was enclosed with a door and a lock, I did not need it.

[25] Before leaving Khon Kaen for Nong Sung, we seriously thought about bringing a stock of bread for Tom. We decided not to because the bus trip did not give us the luxury of having a car carry our luggage from door to door.

The Schoolmaster had retired. Preoccupied with Buddhist religious activities, he frequently made extended trips to various parts of Thailand in pursuit of training in meditation.[26] His wife was often left with the two young helpers and other nearby relatives to keep her company.

Of their nine surviving children, seven—six daughters and one son—were married. All of them had their own children, ranging from one to four in each family and totaling eighteen. During our stay in Khon Kaen, the two unmarried ones, the second son and seventh daughter, also married.

The eldest daughter (D1) lived and worked as a teacher in Roi Et, a provincial town one hour and a half by car from Nong Sung. Her husband was a teacher who, like her own father, became schoolmaster in their district.

The second daughter (D2), a civil servant in Bangkok who had studied sericulture in Japan, headed the Silk Department of the Ministry of Industry. Her husband was Deputy Director of the Bangkok Water Works.

The third daughter (D3), a nurse/administrator at the Ministry of Public Health, was married to a lawyer and lived in Bangkok.

The fourth daughter (D4) ran her own construction company in Bangkok, married a business man, and lived in the capital.

The fifth daughter (D5) married a teacher as her eldest sister (D1) did. A nurse/administrator like the third daughter (D3), she worked at the state hospital in Mukdahan.

Two youngest daughters (D6 and D7), who were young children during Tom's fieldwork, were employed as teachers at the Demonstration School at Khon Kaen University.[27] D6 married a man who was Production Manager in a chicken processing plant near Bangkok which exported its products to Japan. The couple owned a large, Western-style house in Khon Kaen. Because it was not within a walking distance from D6's workplace, the house was occupied only during her husband's occasional visits. For the rest of the time, D6 and her

---

[26] He was ordained as a monk in 1986 and stayed in the monkhood for 6 years until 1992.

[27] It is attached to the University's Faculty of Education and includes kindergarten, elementary school (six years) and junior high school (3 years). Because it offers a good education and many of their alumni pass the entrance examination for prestigious universities, some parents—the third and fifth daughters, for example—send their children to the demonstration school even if they have to live away from home.

son lived with D7 and their two nephews (sons of D3 and D5) in the faculty housing quarters located on campus.

When the youngest daughter (D7) married an electrician in March 1986, we attended the wedding held in her sister's (D6) house in Khon Kaen. Like D6, D7 entered a long-distance marriage; she worked in Khon Kaen and her husband worked in Chiangmai, Northern Thailand. After her marriage, she moved to D6's house and commuted to work by motorcycle.

As with these seven daughters, two sons, who were pupils at the village school in 1963, had established their own careers and lived away from Nong Sung. The older (S1) earned an engineering degree at Khon Kaen University and married a teacher. He worked at a cement firm in Bangkok.

The younger son (S2) majored in political science at college and became a civil servant. In November 1985 while we lived in Khon Kaen, he married a Bangkok woman, a nurse whom he had met at college. We were present at their wedding held in Bangkok. In the same year, he was appointed as Assistant District Officer in his home village, the newly upgraded *king amphoe* (sub-district) headquarters. Thus, their jobs kept this newly-wed couple apart for extended periods.

This brief account of the Schoolmaster's children in 1985-86 illustrates how different their lives had become from those of their parents. First of all, none had stayed in Nong Sung. Though the second son's government post brought him back to his village to live with his parents, it was not a permanent arrangement, for his job involved frequent transfers.

The second difference concerns the children's marriages. The marriage of their parents was village and ethnic endogamy, a common practice in their youth (Kirsch in this volume). Both the Schoolmaster and his wife were Phu Thai, born and raised in Nong Sung. By contrast, none of their children married fellow villagers. Only the third daughter chose a Phu Thai man as her husband, but he was not from Nong Sung. Other children also found their spouses from outside the village. Some (D2, D4, and S2) married Thai from the central region while others (D1, D5, D6 and S1) married Northeasterners. The youngest daughter (D7) chose a man from the North.

Third, in choosing careers, children did not follow the path of their parents. Though the Schoolmaster was an earnest promoter of rural development[28] and keenly aware of the advantages available in the outside world, he was conservative in his choice of occupation. Despite the isolation of Nong Sung in his youth, there were some choices for men which brought them to the wider outside world, while becoming a wife/mother was virtually the only choice available for women (Kirsch in this volume). Yet the Schoolmaster followed in his father's footsteps to become a teacher/farmer and settled in Nong Sung after working at several different schools in the region.

Neither of his sons became a farmer or a teacher, however. Though some of his daughters chose teaching, their father's occupation, none of them married a farmer, not even a part-time one, departing from the path taken by most village women including their own mother. Instead, their education, which was at least as high as college level, led each one of them to establish her own professional career in the much wider society.

In 1985, all the Schoolmaster's children had abandoned agrarian life in their home village and were increasingly incorporated into urban middle-class life. As a result, the family had not only branched out into nine different households, but also was geographically scattered.[29]

Nonetheless, close ties were maintained among its members, creating one big extended family despite the spatial separation. Children visited parents and each other. Parents traveled to see children. In addition, siblings' households provided homes for young children when they attended distant schools. For example, during our stay in Khon Kaen, sons of the third and fifth daughters were studying at the Demonstration School at Khon Kaen University where their two aunts (D6 and D7) were teaching. Since their parents lived in Bangkok and Mukdahan respectively, these two youngsters made their homes at their aunts' house.

No matter where the Schoolmaster's children lived, their ties to Nong Sung remained strong. They "came home" regularly to see their aging parents. For holidays and special rituals, many traveled a long distance to celebrate such occasions in Nong Sung. When we were in the village for *Awk Phansa* (the festival held at the end of the

---

[28] In recognition of his life-long contribution to rural development, the King awarded him a new surname in 1983.

[29] Though it was not uncommon in old days for married children to establish their own household, they normally lived near either husband's or wife's parents. See, for example, Kirsch in this volume.

rainy season) in October 1985 and *Songkhran* (Thai New Year) in April 1986, the Schoolmaster's house was filled with returning children and their families and was lively with various activities. The big two-storied house in the village was still their home.

Nong Sung and the Village Family in 1992

When Tom and I went back to Thailand in 1992, the situation had changed completely. No family member lived in Nong Sung, not even the Schoolmaster and his wife. On our return to the village, we found the family home empty and locked up.[30]

Nong Sung, however, still retained its country charm. The pond and surrounding hills were as beautiful as before. Peace and quietness prevailed in the village, for there was very little vehicular traffic, and trees were throwing inviting shadows on the ground. Living in Bangkok and coping daily with horrendous traffic noise and congestion, we found returning to Nong Sung was like finding an oasis in the desert.

But there were also signs of further development in the village. The dirt road from the bus stop to the center of the village had been paved with bricks, leaving narrow bands of dirt on both sides for pedestrians. Several government offices had been built on the "airfield," a large empty field near the bus stop which in the 1960s was used to graze livestock. These new buildings demonstrated Nong Sung's upgraded status as the *king amphoe* (sub-district) headquarters.

In the six years between 1986 and 1992, Thailand itself had undergone many more changes. Westernized consumer culture and urban life style had become much more prevalent, making enormous impacts on individuals' lives.[31] In 1992, Tom observed his village family as "…for practical purposes completely urban-middle class."[32]

The major change in the Schoolmaster's life had nothing to do with modernization. He had decided to become a Buddhist monk and was ordained in fall 1986 after we left Thailand. In 1992, when

---

[30] During Tom's six-month stay in Bangkok, we went to Khon Kaen for a short time and made a one-day car trip to Nong Sung from there.

[31] Some of these changes are described in footnote #9 in this article (the section on Tom's urban family).

[32] Kirsch 1991.

we visited him, he was living in a village temple a fifteen-minute drive from Nong Sung.

The change in his wife's life, uprooted from her home, was not voluntary. It was caused as much by her husband's monkhood as by the conditions of modern Thailand. After the Schoolmaster became a monk, she lived with her children, rotating among their houses in the Central region and Northeast Thailand. When we saw her in 1992, she was living with the sixth daughter, a teacher, in Khon Kaen. Her old age was very different from that of most rural women in her mother's generation who, even though left alone, remained in their home village, surrounded by children and grandchildren living nearby.

Their nine children continued to live their lives and advance their careers in an urban middle-class setting, experiencing the usual joys, sorrows, and problems of life. There had been three more births in the family: a son for the older son (S1) and two sons for the younger (S2). An unexpected death hit the second daughter's family when one of her four sons was killed in a traffic accident. The long-distance marriage of the sixth daughter in Khon Kaen went on the rocks when she learned that her husband, Production Manager at the Bangkok chicken processing plant, had taken *mie noi,* a second wife.

Nong Sung and the Village Family in 2000

I went to Thailand in early 2000 to place my husband's ashes in Wat Triphun in Nong Sung. During my three-week stay, I saw all the members of Tom's village family except the third daughter. I also had a chance to observe what Thailand had become during my eight-year absence.

Changes that had swept the nation since my last visit in 1992 were beyond my imagination. Walking around Bangkok and traveling around the country, I often wondered what Tom would have said about all these mind-boggling changes. Mushrooming skyscrapers and expressways, for instance, made the Bangkok skyline completely unrecognizable. Sky Train, the city's new mass transit system, ran on highly elevated rails, allowing its passengers to look down on the traffic jams below and enjoy an uninterrupted ride.

Khon Kaen's metamorphosis into a sizable modern city also shocked me, even though I had seen some of its growth on our last visit in 1992. High-rise buildings and bustling traffic dominated the city. Modern shops overflowed into its outskirts, which had been the paddy fields in the mid-eighties. The Khon Kaen that Tom and I had known in 1985-86, a sleepy, provincial center with two major streets running north-south and two east-west, had completely disappeared.

Nong Sung, too, was hit hard by the waves of change. Approaching the village on the two-lane highway, I could barely recognize its bus stop because many more buildings had been built on the "airfield," transforming the once empty land into a government office complex. This notable increase of public offices in the village reflected that Nong Sung had been upgraded from *king amphoe* (sub-district) to *amphoe* (district) in 1993.

To my astonishment, a highway ran through Nong Sung. The road from the bus stop to the center of the village, the main street, had been widened considerably and designated as Route 2370. Like city streets, it was surfaced with asphalt and had concrete side walks on both sides. This cost the loss of half the front yard for the houses along it, including the Schoolmaster's. With big trees cut down and the wooden fence removed, his empty house was exposed to the highway traffic and gave a very different impression from eight years earlier. The national highway through the village and the public office complex at the village entrance indicated that Nong Sung was no longer a marginal community at the periphery of the country but had become a significant part of it.

Cars passed frequently on the highway. Occasionally, villagers' trucks were seen on the narrow, concrete-paved alleys, sharing them with pedestrians and wandering chickens. The pond looked larger than before because retaining walls had been built along its edge to hold more water. At the western end of the pond soared a water supply tower that provided running water to the village households. I noticed many more two-storied houses in the village. Some traditional houses sitting high on poles also gave the appearance of two-storied buildings by enclosing the open space below the floor. There were no high-rise buildings in the village yet.[33] What projected into the sky instead were numerous TV antennas.

The invasion of urban consumer culture into Nong Sung was not limited to television. Upon arrival, we, visitors, were served snacks with

---

[33] By contrast, many high-rise buildings had been built in Mukdahan since my last visit in 1986, transforming a small provincial town into a modern city with a highly visible skyline.

factory-processed bottled water at one of the Schoolmaster's relatives' house. On our previous visits to Nong Sung, we always drank rain water.[34] Recalling the unsure availability of decent drinking water during Tom's fieldwork four decades ago, I thought the bottled water truly symbolized the dramatically altered life in contemporary Nong Sung.

The improvement in telecommunication service in Nong Sung and its vicinity was revolutionary.[35] Communication with the outside world had become so easy that the difficulties Tom had experienced in 1963 were hard to believe.[36] There was a public phone booth in the village and cellular phones were available in the region. The Schoolmaster's family members who traveled with me from Bangkok carried their cellular phones and used them often during our ten-hour drive to Nong Sung.[37] One of their phones rang way out in the country when we were having dinner at a fish restaurant on the banks of the Mekong. This episode epitomized, not only this particular village family's complete assimilation into urban middle-class life, but also the further "mut[ing]" of the "once clear boundary between 'rural' and 'urban' Thailand." [38]

The passage of eight years also brought some major changes to the Schoolmaster's family. His wife died in 1993 at the age of 76. Several years later, his second son, a civil servant, died of heart attack. He was only thirty-seven and left a wife and two young sons behind. The fourth daughter was also widowed when her husband died in his mid-fifties. The youngest (seventh) daughter's long-distance marriage had ended in separation.

---

[34] The tap water in Thailand is not potable, and most people in urban areas buy bottled water to drink. We also drank bottled water in Khon Kaen.

[35] The telephone service in Thailand was far from ideal even in the 1980s. When we lived in Khon Kaen in 1985-86, our phone at home worked only for local calls. When Tom called Bangkok or Chiangmai, he had to go to his office, calling operators and waiting for them to connect him to the other parties, often for a considerable amount of time. We also received many wrong calls because the lines were often crossed. At that time, this problem was so common everywhere in the nation, including Bangkok, that the caller's first words were routinely, "*thi nai*?" or "where is it?," "where did I reach?"

[36] As mentioned earlier, when his mother died, he received a garbled cable and had to make a long journey to Bangkok to call his brother in America.

[37] Two of the daughters (D2 and D4), along with the husband and son of one, accompanied me from Bangkok. Two other daughters (D1 and D5) and their families, who lived within a few hour drive from Nong Sung, also came to the village for the merit-making ceremony for my husband. (On making merit, see Kirsch in this volume.)

[38] Kirsch. Undated.

The Schoolmaster left the monkhood a year before his wife's death. Aged and frail on a wheelchair but keen in mind, he now lives in Bangkok, rotating among his children's homes every two to three weeks. Boredom, children said, prompts him to move from one household to another.

Though two of his children, the first and second daughters, have retired, the rest pursue their careers as before. The second son's widow lives in Bangkok, her home town, with her two sons. She continues to work as a nurse and runs a gift shop with her sister.

Most of the Schoolmaster's twenty grandchildren are old enough to go to college, have their own careers, or even get married.[39] In this generation, the family's separation from their Phu Thai roots is more apparent. None of them grew up in Nong Sung. They know village life only through occasional visits there and stories about it. They understand simple Phu Thai but cannot speak it. Instead, they speak Thai and some also speak English.

They belong to the well-educated urban middle-class. Firmly anchored there, their primary goal is not becoming integrated into the national system as was their parents' but doing well in it. One possible strategy for success is to expand their world beyond the boundary of Thailand, as many Thais of this social class (e.g., Lek and his son in Tom's urban family) have done.

The Schoolmaster's family has been following the right path in this regard. As noted earlier, the second daughter studied in Japan on a government scholarship. In the succeeding generation, one of the third daughter's sons is studying for an advanced degree in an Australian university. The fourth daughter's elder son worked for a French company and switched to a Japanese company just before my visit to Thailand. His former job involved international travel. The oldest son of the Schoolmaster's first son is coming to the United States to work for the Disney Corporation in the near future. The lives of the Schoolmaster's grandchildren clearly show the remarkable influence of the globalization on the family.[40]

---

[39] The Schoolmaster had a total of 21 grandchildren. But, as mentioned above, one of them, the second daughter's son, was killed in a traffic accident. He has two great-grandchildren.

[40] As in the case of Tom's urban family, e-mail facilitates the village family's expansion into the global stage. One of the schoolmaster's grandchildren, for instance, is in touch with me in America via e-mail.

At the same time, the postmortem treatment of their grandmother, the Schoolmaster's wife, reflects not only the family's continuing ties to Nong Sung but also their settlement in the urban area. After an elaborate funeral and cremation in Bangkok, her ashes were placed in a Bangkok temple rather than Wat Triphun in Nong Sung where the deceased, a pious Buddhist, had long assumed a leadership role among village women.

The remains of the Schoolmaster's wife found an eternal home in Bangkok. Yet, it is at Wat Triphun in Nong Sung where a marble plate with her picture, her name, and the dates of her birth and death was inlaid on the wall of one of the temple buildings. This special privilege was accorded her, not only because her family made an unusually large donation (47,000 Baht or over $1200) to the village temple to make merit for her, but also because the family still retains in absentia the influence and respect in the village community.[41]

Four Decades of Changes

In the early 1960s, my husband found Nong Sung "[had] changed and [was] changing: becoming more 'Thai-icized' and more 'Buddha-ized'"[42] despite the ethnic separation villagers maintained both from their Thai-Lao neighbors and from the Thai of the Central region. Observing that the Thai culture entering the village was the "national culture emanating from Bangkok,"[43] he predicted:

> ...in becoming "Thai-icized," Nong Sung is not becoming more like the farming villages of the Central region. It is becoming more like a Thai town or city. Many young villagers have a vision of a future Nong Sung which they express in idle talk and fantasy. This vision is of paved streets and automobiles, of electricity and television, or movie houses, stores, and markets. That is, they envisage the Nong Sung of the future with urban trappings.[44]

---

[41] Thanks to their connection to the Nong Sung community, my husband's *chedi*, a stupa, was placed inside the village temple compound, a privilege normally reserved only for deceased ordained monks.

[42] Kirsch in this volume, p. 3, 54, and 56.

[43] ibid., p. 57.

[44] ibid., p. 57.

Except for movie houses and markets, what was a pure fantasy four decades ago has become a reality in today's Nong Sung. The Schoolmaster, his wife, and their nine children have lived through these massive changes, successfully adapting to them and extending their horizon to include the national and global stages.

Conclusion

Doing fieldwork is a rite of passage for anthropologists. We attempt to learn another culture from within by living among the people under study for a prolonged period of time. Though ethnographies are normally silent about their authors, fieldwork often involves various physical, emotional, and intellectual challenges, as well documented by Bronislaw Malinowski who established long-term participant-observation as an anthropological research method.[45] Not surprisingly, experiences in the field have strong, lasting impacts on the researcher in both personal and professional terms.

This was the case with Tom. His fieldwork in Nong Sung in the early 1960s certainly was not easy. Among other things, tropical sprue put his life in danger. Yet, he wrote in one of his letters from the field:

> I suppose that I will follow the same pattern as Evans-Pritchard. In his first book about the Nuer he complained about the dirty surly savages. In his latest book (20 plus years later) he glows over their fine philosophical insights. In a few years I will get misty eyed over shaving in cold water, the monotony and dreary sameness of the food.[46]

He prophesied correctly. For almost four decades until his death, Thailand occupied a special place in his heart. Thus, he wished his ashes to be buried in his field site, Nong Sung. Undoubtedly, Tom's two Thai families contributed to this special feeling he had for Thailand. The village family provided him with a home, mitigated his hardships, and helped facilitate his research. Similarly, the urban family became Tom's Bangkok home when he needed a break from the rigors of upcountry living. They even assisted him with his visa problems.[47]

---

[45] Bronislaw Malinowski. 1989 (1967). *A Diary in the Strict Sense of the Term*. Stanford: Stanford University Press.

[46] Kirsch 1963 (July 15).

[47] In the same letter mentioned above, Tom asked Charles Keyes who had just returned from Bangkok to his field site in Northeast Thailand, "Was Bangkok still as wonderful as I remember it? Of course it was."

Thailand also carried much intellectual significance for Tom. It gave him an opportunity to collect empirical data and connect them to social theories. This in turn enabled him to explore the relationship between the concrete and the abstract and to narrow the gap between them. Theravada Buddhism, the belief system at the core of Thai culture, enhanced Tom's understanding of religion and theories about it. In addition, Thailand allowed Tom to witness, "extraordinary changes" during four decades of his academic career, offering him a valuable "laboratory" for testing his temporally dynamic view of human life. Tom's two Thai families played an essential role in his last research to explore "the qualitative and human effects of the profound changes" on the lives of individuals as well as to consider what their lives would be like in the future.[48]

I once asked Tom why he chose to study Thailand. Instead of a straightforward answer, he told me how his interest in geography led him to anthropology and then, with a smile on his face, said, "It was karma." Surrounded by more than four scores of Tom's Thai "relatives" and friends at Nong Sung's Wat Triphun during the merit-making ceremony for him, I could think of no better explanation than karma for his, and my, encounter with these two extraordinary Thai families.

2007 Epilogue

In November 2007, I returned to Thailand in the midst of an election campaign and the preparation for the King's 80th birthday. During my brief stay, I saw the members of both the urban family and the village family, revisited Nong Sung, and witnessed even more transformations in the Kingdom than in 2000. Many changes also occurred to my husband's two Thai families in those seven years.

The Urban Family in 2007

The primary change in Lek's family was his son's marriage in 2006. It was a two-career marriage with both the husband and the wife working as faculty members at Chulalongkorn University. Their living arrangement, however, did not follow the neo-local residence young Thai couples prefer today. Instead, upon marriage, the bride

---

[48] Kirsch 1991.

moved in with the groom's family to live with her husband and his parents. While the bride worked full time, her mother-in-law took care of domestic chores. Undoubtedly, this arrangement was advantageous for a two-career marriage, though some other factors might have also contributed to their decision.

After the son's marriage, the headship of the household was transferred from the father to the son. Lek was in good health thanks to his daily walking and was enjoying his retirement. The son's marriage enabled his wife to enjoy her favorite pastime, shopping in the heart of Bangkok, without Lek accompanying her. She took the train into town and returned home with the young couple in their car. Sometimes, the mother-in-law and the daughter-in-law went shopping together.

Lek's son's career advanced smoothly. In addition to teaching physics, he assumed the position of the Deputy Dean in 2007. His job also included attending and organizing international conferences. Furthermore, every two years, the exchange program required him to spend several months at a Swedish university where he had received his Ph.D. and post-doctoral training. Japan, where his wife earned her Ph.D. in chemistry, became another regular destination of this young couple. Thus, even though they continued to reside in Thailand, their career had a global stage.

The Village Family in 2007

In November 2007, I attended the wedding of one of the Schoolmaster's grandsons in Bangkok and had a reunion with his children and grandchildren. Immediately apparent was the demographic change in this family. First of all, the Schoolmaster had passed away in 2001, a year after I saw him in Bangkok. The second was the retirement of his children. Of the eight surviving children (the second son had died in the 1990s), all but the first son and the seventh (youngest) daughter had retired.

Many grandchildren had married and become parents, which further increased the family size. The Schoolmaster's grandchildren also advanced their careers and came to assume significant positions in the urban, non-agricultural occupations. Whereas their parents successfully made the transition from the rural agrarian lifestyle to the urban middle-class one, they grew up in urban areas without knowing farming life in Nong Sung and without speaking Phu Thai, the local language.

Among other things, the 2007 wedding of the Schoolmaster's grandson reflected the tremendous changes that had occurred in Thailand as well as to the Schoolmaster's family since my first trip to the Kingdom in 1985. The wedding started early in the morning with a Buddhist ritual.[49] Half a dozen monks chanted sutras and gave blessings to the newly weds. At the end of this ritual, monks received the offering of gift and food. Afterwards, the feasting for lay attendees started.

This ritual and feast were similar to those my husband and I had participated in when the Schoolmaster's younger son married in Bangkok in 1985 and his youngest daughter in Khon Kaen in 1986. However, the site of the 2007 ceremony revealed how urban and middle-class this family had become. Both the ritual and the feast were held at the home of the groom and the bride in a gated-community in one of the Bangkok suburbs. At the gate were security guards who allowed visitors in only after checking who they were, whom they were visiting, and whether the residents had requested for their entry. The entire compound was beautifully landscaped and meticulously maintained. The two-storied house of the newly-weds had a carport and a small yard with lawn. Inside were a modern kitchen, a multitude of appliances, and Western-style furniture and bathrooms. Their home reminded me of the pictures of suburban housing estates which my husband had taken in 1992 when many of them were being built and advertised for sale.[50]

Another difference between the 2007 wedding and the two in the 1980s was found in *su khwan*, the soul-tying ceremony of tying threads around wrists. Not only was it "the central focus of the mar-

---

[49] It is customary to do so because Buddhist monks are not allowed to eat after noon. However, this custom was relatively recently established. My husband noted in the 1960s, "[M]onks never even attend weddings in Nong Sung" (Kirsch in this volume, p. 35).

[50] The sixth daughter also moved to a gated community in Khon Kaen located several miles from downtown. The scale of her community was much smaller than that of her nephew's in Bangkok although her equally modern house was larger than her nephew's. There, the security check at the gate was cursory; the guard simply opened it when the driver stopped a car. In addition, a few residents converted a part of their houses into convenience stores where other residents in the community picked up their necessities without going into town.

riage ceremony" in Nong Sung in the 1960s,[51] but its significance also remained in the 1980s weddings, in which both the newly-weds and relatives and guests, including Tom and me, had their wrists tied with many threads. By contrast, at the 2007 wedding, only the bride and the groom received the thread from a small number of well-wishers.

The most striking difference of the 2007 wedding from the two previous ones is that the former had a second part, an evening reception with more than three hundred guests.[52] The bride wore a Western-style wedding gown and the groom a tuxedo, although both were clad in the formal Thai outfit at the morning Buddhist ceremony. Chinese dinner was served while pictures of the bride and the groom and American music videos were screened. The master of ceremonies, another grandson of the Schoolmaster (the groom's cousin), invited some guests to the stage to give a speech. Among them was the groom's boss, one of the two Westerners on the scene. He made his speech in English, which the MC translated into Thai. None of these had occurred at the two previous weddings of the Schoolmaster's children in the 1980s. The addition of this reception, which was held in a popular wedding hall in one of the Bangkok skyscrapers, revealed the commercialization of Thai weddings. The heightened consumerism among urban Thai middle-class was also apparent in the huge multi-level parking garage overfilled with cars, as well as in one of the luxurious Western-style apartments in the building, which was assigned to the wedding party for getting dressed and resting.

In addition to commercialization and consumerism, globalization had a significant impact on this family. This was more common among the Schoolmaster's grandchildren, although his second daughter had studied sericulture in Japan in her youth and his first son traveled abroad on business. The groom of the 2007 wedding, for example, had a master's degree from an Australian university and worked for a foreign company in Bangkok. Hence, two Westerners, his boss and one of his colleagues, attended the wedding reception. In 2007, his brother and his parents (third daughter and her husband) stayed in America for an extended period to help his paternal uncle's

---

[51] Kirsch in this volume, p. 35.

[52] Such a two-part wedding has become popular among urban Thais. When the son of the urban family got married, his wedding also had a reception in addition to a morning Buddhist ceremony. However, due to his work schedule as well as of his bride's, these two parts were held on two separate days.

restaurant business in New Jersey. Another grandson (the eldest of the Schoolmaster's first son) had spent a year in America to work at Disney World. Back in Bangkok, he ran a computer company that had customers and business associates inside and outside of Thailand.[53]

Nong Sung and Khon Kaen had changed enormously in seven years. Khon Kaen looked like a small metropolis with a good number of high-rise buildings and highways. Along the highways were car dealers with big signs saying Toyota, Isuzu, and Nissan. The metamorphosis of Khon Kaen University was equally amazing. Multi-storied buildings had sprung up everywhere, and two-lane highways ran through the campus. Comparing two *Loy Kratong*, the lantern festival, held on campus in 1985 and 2007 made me realize the enormity of the changes, in particular, the increasing significance of consumerism in the outer areas of the nation.

The *Loy Kratong* in 1985 was a simple affair. A group of people gathered at the faculty club, floated lit-lanterns on the 25-meter swimming pool, played music, and sang together the *Loy Kratong* song over snacks and drinks. The 2007 celebration was a completely different matter. It attracted a huge crowd and a vast number of cars. Many vendors sold ritual necessities, such as candles, lanterns, and wreaths, as well as foods, toys, gift items, and clothing. The reservoir where people floated their lanterns was many times larger than the 25-meter pool. But the number of lanterns on it was so great that several young men were standing in the water to move them away from the shore. At the new outdoor theater, where the commencement was held annually, attractions were going on to entertain a big audience with music, dancing, and a beauty contest. Literally, every place at the expansive festival site was packed with people.

Changes in Nong Sung were also remarkable. The sign on the highway clearly indicated Nong Sung's administrative status of *amphoe* (district) headquarters. Upon arrival, I discovered that a permanent market had opened at the west end of the village near the bus stop. Many vendors filled the concrete building, selling meat, vegetables, fruit, cooked food, clothing, china, kitchen utensils, and other daily necessities. Some of these goods came from foreign countries. For

---

[53] In 2008, this grandson received a scholarship for the MBA program at KAIST (formerly the Korea Advanced Institute of Science and Technology). He studied at the KAIST Business School in Seoul for a year and participated in the summer program for KAIST students at the University of Southern California in 2009.

instance, apples and grapes from Australia were sold next to various domestic fruit. When my husband and I lived in Khon Kaen in 1985-86, these were expensive fruits available only at upscale stores in Bangkok.

The distance between Nong Sung and the rest of the world had narrowed in other ways. There was an internet cafe on the main street, which I had found in 2000 transformed into Route 2370. Beyond the village water-supply tower rose two much taller cellular phone towers. These additions instantaneously connected villagers to anywhere in the world. It was hard to believe that most houses in Nong Sung, including the Schoolmaster's, did not have a regular phone service as recently as the 1980s. Vehicular accessibility to Nong Sung also had improved tremendously. The drive from Khon Kaen took hardly two hours and was on four-lane highways except for the last short stretch of two-lane highway.

All these changes might echo the social change that had swept Thailand in recent years. Among other things, the East-West Corridor Project involving Thailand, Laos, Vietnam accelerated the development of Northeast Thailand. For instance, the Project brought to the region many new and expanded highways as well as the Friendship Bridge over the Mekong river near Mukdahan that enabled car traffic between Thailand and Laos.

These changes were epitomized in the French bread served at the breakfast table at the fifth daughter's house in Mukdahan. It was freshly baked by a Vietnamese baker in town and tasted better than the French bread I could obtain in Ithaca, New York. No wonder this was her husband's favorite breakfast. During my husband's initial fieldwork, bread was not available in the region. Only once in a great while he enjoyed the French bread villagers brought back from Laos by crossing the Mekong by boat.

Although the most important highways did not run through Nong Sung, the waves of development had had strong impacts on the villagers' life style. These waves did not leave out the village *wat* (temple), either. Since my previous visit in 2000, a drum tower had been built with the contribution of the Schoolmaster's family. To make room for it, some big trees had been cut and all the *chedi* (stupas), including that of my husband, had been relocated along the fence. In addition, a large multi-storied building was under construction. When completed, it would serve not only as living quarters for the resident monks and the visiting clergy, but also as a regional meditation center.

The biggest, and most shocking, change for me personally was the demolition of the Schoolmaster's house. Although the property, co-owned by the first, forth, and seventh daughters, still belonged to the family, all that remained was a pile of teak planks from the old house. This house had been sitting empty for nearly two decades and needed much repair. It also lacked much of what urban Thai houses have today, such as flush toilets and private bedrooms. Because there was no prospect of any of the Schoolmaster's children and grandchildren living there in the near future, demolition made more sense than spending money on repair or renovation. Even so, it was sad to see the old house gone. As one of the two two-storied houses in the village in the early 1960s when the rest of the village houses stood on high poles with a loom and a couple of water buffalos beneath them, the Schoolmaster's house symbolized the modernity of the era. Its history and its demolition told us the immense social and economic transformations in Nong Sung and in his family.

In the midst of enormous changes, however, the family legacy and the family ties to their place of origin continued. Despite the fact that none of the Schoolmaster's children and grandchildren chose agriculture as their profession, cultivating the land seemed to interest some of his descendants. A good example of this is the sixth daughter. Although she lived in a Western-style house in a gated community in Khon Kaen, she grew potatoes at a nearby farm she had bought after retirement. The love of growing things was passed down to the next generation as well. The eldest son of the Schoolmaster's first son had a farm in Loei Province. A bachelor in his twenties, he worked in computer business in Bangkok but frequently visited his farm by car or by plane.

There was a possibility that a family member would start living in Nong Sung again. The Schoolmaster's youngest daughter contemplated her retirement in Nong Sung. Divorced without children, she regarded it a good plan to return to her birthplace, build a house on the land she co-owned with her two elder sisters, and spend her later years there. Until her plan materialized, it was most unlikely that any descendants of the Schoolmaster would be living in Nong Sung. But even in absentia, the family's presence was evident in the village. The drum tower, their donation, at the temple unmistakably represented it. In addition, a plaque of the Schoolmaster's picture with his name and birth and death dates was built in on the temple wall next to that of his wife, even though their ashes were placed in a *wat* in the Bangkok suburbs near the third daughter's house.

Conclusion

When my husband first went to Thailand in 1962, the Kingdom was vastly different from what it is today. To compare the Bangkok from the time of his first trip to that of his last in 1992, he often used an anecdote about the city's traffic. In the early days, he could cross the street without fearing a car would run over him. In 1978, he waited for monks to come and crossed the street with them because, he thought, no Thai driver would wish to kill the Buddhist clergy. On his last two trips, this trick ceased to work and the only safe way to cross the street was using an overhead bridge.

Nong Sung had changed so immensely merely in one generation (i.e., that of the Schoolmaster's children) that Tom did not have just one illustrative story to tell. In the early 1960s, it had neither electricity nor running water. It also lacked postal service and all-weather roads. The absence of these two facilities, coupled with its peripheral location, made communication with the outside world difficult. Nonetheless, Tom saw the seeds of change in this remote village. He wrote that Nong Sung was not only "becoming a part of the larger and more inclusive social world"[54] but also "becoming more like a Thai town or city" rather than a farming village of the Central region.[55] On my visit to Nong Sung in 2000, I discovered that the Nong Sung envisaged four decades ago had become a reality except for a market and a movie theater. In 2007, I saw that a market had materialized.

Many changes also occurred to my husband's two Thai families. Some of them can be attributed to the developmental cycle of the family, such as the growth and the marriage of children, the passing of the parental generation, and the birth of grandchildren. In the urban family, the death of the matriarch led to the dissolution of the extended family and the creation of Lek's nuclear family in the suburbs. The

---

[54] Kirsch in this volume, p. 54.

[55] ibid., p. 57.

decreasing size of the village family was already notable when Tom lived in their house in the early 1960s although none of the School-master's nine children was married. His older children had left home, not to start their own families, but "to acquire advanced education and to enter national channels of mobility."[56] All of them succeeded in their pursuit and became assimilated into the urban middle-class.

As a channel of mobility, education continued to play a sig-nificant role in the succeeding generation of both families. In addi-tion, education outside of Thailand became increasingly important. Studying abroad was not unknown to these two families even when it was beyond the reach of most Thai. Lek studied in Germany and the Schoolmaster's second daughter in Japan.[57] However, the degree to which the two families are integrated into the globalized world through education and occupation is much greater today. Many more members of these families, especially those in the younger generation, speak English, some fluently. As my Thai had become rusty, English replaced Thai as the sole language of my communication with these two families.

During my stay in Thailand in 2007, an unprecedented event occurred. My husband's two Thai families met for the first time. All four members of the urban family and one nuclear unit of the vil-lage family—the Schoolmaster's older son, his wife, their sons—met on the campus of Chulalongkorn University. Their chance encounter made me ponder about karma. For what else could I think of that con-nected Tom's two Thai families, these families with him and later with me, and finally Tom and me, who were born and raised thousands of miles apart in two different countries?

---

[56] Kirsch in this volume, p. 54.

[57] In addition to the Schoolmaster's second daughter, a Nong Sung man went to America to earn an M.A. prior to my husband's fieldwork (Kirsch in this volume, p. 43). Moreover, visiting a foreign country was a routine event in Nong Sung's past when cattle trade required village men travel as far away as to Burma (Kirsch in this volume, p. 8).

A Memoir[1]

O. W. Wolters [2]

Anthony Thomas Kirsch, a distinguished student of Thai Buddhism, Professor of Anthropology and Asian Studies, and a member of the Cornell Southeast Asia Program since 1970, died on 17 May, 1999.

He was born in Syracuse, New York, on 29 May, 1930, into a family that, on his father's side, came from Germany. His mother was Florence Sheehan; her family was Irish. His grandfather owned a large dairy, dairy shop, and potato farm on land that included or was near the site of Syracuse's Hancock International Airport. Tom and his cousins would be recruited to help harvest potatoes, and he is remembered as a somewhat reluctant toiler on the land; sometimes his absence was noticed and he would be found reading in an apple tree. Working in the yard never became one of his preoccupations in later life.

He was brought up in a devout Catholic family that donated land in Mattydale for the original St. Margaret's Church and convent and also the first public library in the area.[3] His relatives were numerous. They farmed together and went to the same schools. Each summer they still celebrate reunions of a hundred or more of all ages on the shores of Onondaga Lake, where their custom is to consume half an ox. Tom and Yohko, his wife, habitually attended these gatherings. In his pre-Harvard days he was regarded as being quiet and reserved, though he also fancied himself behind the wheel of an MG. His relatives may never have quite understood their eccentric kinsman and why, when a student at Harvard, he should have decided to go to the other end of the world and live in a Thai village.

---

[1] I thank a number of Tom's friends, and especially his wife, Yohko Kirsch Tsuji. Without their willing assistance, this memoir could not have been written.

[2] At the time of writing this essay, Oliver W. Wolters was Goldwin Smith Professor Emeritus of History and Asian Studies at Cornell University. Born and raised in Great Britain, he used the British spellings and punctuations, which are left intact. Oliver passed away in December 2000. "A Memoir" was originally published in the *Bulletin* of the Cornell Southeast Asia Program and is reprinted here by permission (footnote added by Yohko Tsuji).

[3] For these and other historical details concerning Mattydale, see Helen Burnham, Trolley Stops Two, Three, & Four (Baldwinsville, New York, Eagle Media, Inc., 1994).

He was educated at the Christian Brothers Academy, Syracuse, and received what today would be regarded as a traditional education. He studied "Religion" and "English" for four years, "History" for three, and "Latin" for one. Unfortunately, in view of what lay ahead for him, details about the range of his religious studies are not available. His parents urged him to read as much as possible and consider a career away from the farm. After leaving school and spending a year as an "inspector" on an assembly line in a factory producing TV sets (one of the first of its kind), he decided to become an electrical engineer, but soon realised that he had no mathematical and calculus skills. He then considered a career in professional geography, entered Syracuse University, was advised to study some anthropology, and became "enraptured", as he wrote years later, and now knew where his interests lay. Administrative circumstances required him to take a joint anthropology/sociology major, with a fateful consequence; he was introduced to the influential theoretical work of Talcott Parsons and a number of issues such as sex roles and kinship that were one day to occupy his attention.

He received a B.A. *cum laude* in 1952, was drafted into the U.S. Army, and there he undertook medical and psychiatric work from 1953 to 1955. He recalled many years later that his military experience provided him with an environment in which he could read and study cultural, social, and psychological matters. Thereafter, having worked briefly in his family's business, he returned to Syracuse University because he knew that academe was where he really wanted to be. He took an M.A. in 1959 before proceeding to Harvard for graduate studies in anthropology.[4] His earliest connection with Cornell was in 1961-1962, when he began studying the Thai language. Unfortunately, why Thailand should have been his country of choice is not known for certain, though the choice had been made before he went to Harvard. He once disclosed that he was fascinated by Thailand's geographical shape and especially by how it lunged into southern

---

[4] His M.A. thesis was on "Factors Influencing the Relations of Married Siblings". It was basically a sociological one and somewhat influenced by Talcott Parsons's essay on social stratification in industrial societies. Noting the interesting circumstance that a brother of the head of General Motors had been employed in that firm as an hourly paid worker, he developed the hypothesis that the more divergent the status difference was in occupational terms the less close ties would be between close relatives. He conducted his research among members of the "wives" club of the engineering staff of a large manufacturing plant in the area.

China and the Malay Peninsula. Geography had been one of his earliest adult interests.

He would have arrived in Cambridge feeling independent as never before. He was probably unusually well educated, inquisitive, and with plenty of ideas in his head. His fellow graduates remember him, as we who knew him subsequently do, as a friend who gladly shared his knowledge with anyone who talked to him. He had come to Harvard at an exciting time in the history of social anthropology, when the dynamic relation of culture and society was a focus of enquiry. He had already been influenced by Talcott Parsons's emphasis on social systems and their dependence on cultural orientations, and he became convinced, as he later wrote in his classic *Feasting and Social Oscillation: Religion and Society in Upland Southeast Asia,* "that religion is the repository of cultural values and conceptions which provide the cognitive and effective framework within which social action takes place."[5] This view was being taught at Harvard when Tom was there, and his achievement later would be to elaborate it in the context of Theravada Buddhism in Thailand, the core beliefs of which he knew thoroughly.[6] A fellow anthropologist has praised Tom's success in being able to link Parsonian theory with empirical data.

His lifelong intellectual concerns were announced in a daringly ambitious doctoral outline of May 1964, pruned to become a study of Phu Thai religious syncretism in northeastern Thailand. During 1962-1964 he lived with a village schoolmaster in Ban Nong Sung, a remote and largely unknown village in the District of Khamcha-ee and in what today is the province of Mukdahan. A few years ago an old monk in Washington, D.C. recalled how Tom—the only Westerner not only in the village but in that part of the northeast as well—had impressed the population. Perhaps his youthful years on a farm in

[5] A. Thomas Kirsch, *Feasting and Social Oscillation: Religion and Society in Upland Southeast Asia.* [Data Paper 92], (Ithaca, Cornell University Southeast Asia Program, July 1973), 3. Professor James L. Peacock, speaking during the symposium in Tom's honour, held in February, 1999, suggested that Tom's understanding of the influence of Theravada Buddhism on Thai women was "unequalled in demonstrating the force of religion in the social order".

[6] His spirited reaffirmation of what he regarded as Thai gender roles relied to a significant extent on his ability to gloss the Thai "Blessings of Ordination" text in order to read it as encoding Theravada teachings. He rejected the suggestion that, in Buddhist terms, anyone could be "naturally good". All were human beings caught up in a world of ignorance, desire, and illusion ("Text and Context: Buddhist sex-roles/cultures of gender revisited", *American Ethnologist* 12, 2 [1985], 306).

upstate New York helped him settle down in the Thai countryside, and his Catholic upbringing may have accustomed him to a way of life that respected authority, discipline, and ritual, and enabled him to understand similar elements in the Theravada Buddhist way of life practised in his village. At any rate, his affection for his village meant that thereafter he was always eager to teach that the surest basis for ethically grounded conduct was village Buddhism rather than the rational Buddhism of the metropolis or versions of Buddhism without "Asian trappings" which usually appealed to Westerners. The village of Ban Nong Sung became the personal adventure and intellectual influence that remained with him until the end. Unless his village is borne in mind, not much sense can be made of Tom's subsequent life.

His doctoral outline, written after he returned from Thailand with tropical sprue, reads today as though he was already drawing up the research programme that occupied him throughout his career. It comprised no less than the study of the hill tribes of mainland Southeast Asia, the "sanskritic" peoples of the lowlands of mainland Southeast Asia, and the Theravada Buddhist countries of Southeast Asia. Not surprising, the outline was more than thirty pages in length.

Still at Harvard, he wrote graduate papers on these topics against the day when he could return to them, as indeed he did. Professor Hjorleifur Jonsson, who came to Cornell because he was attracted by Tom's interest in the highland peoples of mainland Southeast Asia and was among the last students to complete a doctoral dissertation under his supervision, is introducing a collection of Tom's influential writings for publication under SEAP [Southeast Asia Program] auspices. Two items remain unpublished. The collection will illustrate the range and coherence of Tom's intellectual preoccupations and also how he approached Southeast Asia as a field of study. In several instances he seems to have anticipated research directions anthropologists followed later.

The writer of this memoir owed Tom much. Tom honoured him by attending and participating in his lectures and sought to persuade him that there was more to be done to "history" when cultural and social influences were borne in mind. He was a historian's anthropologist. There he was continually at one's side, quietly proposing, by way of speculation or hypothesis, new ways of looking at the past and advancing reasons for doing so as a result of his anthropological insights. Three of the essays in the projected collection of his works concern Thai and Khmer history, and they read, among other things, as written from the perspective of a scholar alert for signs of movement and maybe change beneath what he called the "surface" of a text.[7] In his essays on history he mobilised his anthropological expertise to challenge conventional wisdom on, for example, the significance of kinship systems or on the rise and fall of cultural and social systems. He paid attention to contingencies such as warfare, succession disputes, and manpower needs rather than following rigid models of social organisation. He always sought to identify human agency and motivation as factors influencing the course of events.

With a lifetime of research goals in his notebooks, he left Harvard in 1966 to become an assistant professor at Princeton and worked there until, in 1970, he began his Cornell career of nearly thirty years, where by all accounts he undertook every responsibility that could be asked of him, and had the reputation of volunteering to do whatever needed to be done.[8] Only a year after arriving, he had already begun to serve the first of three terms as chairman of the anthropology department and by 1990 had completed more than nine years of service.[9] Those close to him remember that he managed to take the ups and downs of office in his stride and always with a twinkle in his eye. He served on heaps of departmental committees. Some will remember him as having a propensity for dashing off on his typewriter ("no infernal word-processor for me") long and forcefully argued memoranda addressed to those in authority whom he thought had treated his department without proper consideration.[10] Yet he seems to have been the obvious choice for a series of college deans when they had to

---

[7] Language such as "responsible", "actor", "activating", "mobilizing", "achieving", "valuing", "rewarding", "promoting", "punishing", "recruiting," "had to resort to", "staking a claim", and "calling on to support" signify the matter-of-fact but actual happenings that interested him.

[8] He rallied behind the author's ineffectual attempt to organise an interregional and multidisciplinary seminar. An extract from his presentation will appear in Professor Jonsson's collection of Tom's works.

[9] He served briefly as acting chairman of the Department of Asian Studies.

[10] One day, strolling back to McGraw Hall with him after a SEAP meeting, the author told him casually that he had recently noticed a favourable review of a certain book by an anthropologist. Within half an hour Tom dumped a three-page note on the author's desk to warn him of the book's harmful tendencies.

appoint faculty members to serve on committees. From time to time he was a member of the Faculty Council of Representatives. And this is not the limit of his miscellaneous services to the academic community. In 1989 he was one of several scholars asked to create a program for the study of religion at Cornell. He served on the program's steering committee until his death and chaired its curriculum committee. At the same time he lectured on "Magic, Myth, Science, and Religion".

As a member of the Executive Committee of the Southeast Asia Program, he would exhibit his familiarity with the regulations of the college and his expert experience with the moods and whims of deans. When necessary, according to a colleague, he would utter the group's conscience and remind it of what it was supposed to be do-ing. He was a stickler for the rules of academic life. He made himself responsible for organising the annual film series on Southeast Asia. But, much more important, he was a favourite chairman of graduate committees and was also in demand as a "minor" member of these committees.[11] He sponsored the publication of manuscripts written by scholars visiting the program and wrote forewords and prefaces for them. He coedited a *festschrift* in honour of Lauriston Sharp, the program's founder, and cooperated in planning a *festschrift* in honour of Jane and Lucien Hanks. Away from Cornell, he served on the Thai-land Council of the Asia Society and the Southeast Asian Council of the Association for Asian Studies (AAS). Between 1965 and 1992 he attended numerous seminars, symposiums, and panels organised by the American Anthropological Association, the Association of Asian Studies, the Asia Society, and centers of learning in various parts of the country and in Thailand. He regularly wrote book reviews. From time to time he refereed book manuscripts and journal articles. In 1985-1986 he served as a Fulbright scholar and consultant at Khon Kaen University, Thailand. In 1992, he received a Fulbright Hays Fac-ulty Research Abroad Award and became a Visiting Senior Scholar at the Chulalongkorn University Social Research Institute.

In 1984 he married Yohko Tsuji, a fellow anthropologist and a joy to him as well as a helpmate in times of need if ever there was one. They were a happy, hospitable pair. She amused him, as he did her. They were together in Thailand in 1985-1986 and 1992. On the

---

[11] Four of his students were awarded "Lauriston Sharp" prizes for scholarly excellence. He served on the committees of six other prize winners. The prize was established in 1975, and Tom was closely involved with a third of the prize winners.

latter occasion, Tom was preparing materials for a "Social History of Two Thai Families: 1960-1990", concerning the families with whom he had kept in touch since his Harvard days. His intention was to gauge the qualitative and human effects of the profound changes that had occurred in Thailand during this period. But he returned from his last visit to Thailand in discomfort, and shortly afterwards, in October, 1992, his larynx had to be removed. The disaster occurred only two years after he had given up the chairmanship of his department, and he had been looking forward to fewer duties. He now had to converse by means of an electrolarynx. For a less brave man, the disaster could have meant the end of a useful career, but the contrary happened. Without showing a trace of self-pity even when he was often required to undergo further and disagreeable medical treatment in Syracuse, and supported by his courageous wife, Tom responded to his predicament with admirable endurance and carried on uncomplainingly. He may even have been grateful that he was still a teacher and student advisor and relieved at last of what he was to describe as "extraordinary administrative responsibilities that adversely influence my time, thought, and energy". In his last years he was perhaps at peace professionally as never before and could write that "I know that I enjoy my teaching and advising more now than I did previously". He never behaved as though he were handicapped. His colleagues readily took his composure for granted, and he wanted nothing else.

With a new "voice", and determined to be active, he was now known to be almost furiously busy lecturing and revising lectures to make them, he said, more relevant to the state of contemporary theory and the state of regional developments. At the same time, he was always seeing students, holding examinations, and attending endless departmental meetings. As a result of this sudden whirl of activity, his friends often found it difficult to get in touch with him. In 1994-1995 he took a great deal of trouble to compose an authoritative and affectionate memorial statement in honour of Lauriston Sharp, whom he admired and often quoted. In 1995 he participated in conferences in Leiden and Lund and was a panel discussant at the 1995 and 1996 AAS meetings in Hawaii and Washington, D.C. In 1997 he travelled in the British Isles and visited Oxford, where he enjoyed examining the "utterly overpowering" Pitt-Rivers Ethnological Museum. In 1997 he accompanied Yohko to Japan. Also in these post-1992 years, his resolve to carry on in spite of his disability meant that he grasped an opportunity to return with passion to an earlier intellectual interest, which was a concern for the future. The opportunity, as we shall see, came in the form of the Southeast Asia Program's "Golay Memorial Lectures".

Tom's concern with the future was derived from his long-standing interest in the past and, therefore, with what came next. When travelling in Britain, he was well-informed about and relished heritage sites. Three articles in the projected collection for his writings are on historical subjects. Perhaps his interest was originally awakened as a result of his education at the Christian Brothers Academy in Syracuse. Certainly long ago at Harvard he had encouraged his peers not to neglect history.[12] His doctoral outline included what he called "an evolutionary dimension" and involved a detailed historical approach to the "sanskritic" civilisations. Not many years later he coauthored *The Human Direction: An Evolutionary Introduction to Social and Cultural Anthropology*.[13] History and evolution seem to have been interchangeable notions.

His interest in history also led him to study the history of his discipline, and this had become a sufficiently lively interest that he spent 1974-1975 at the Peabody Museum at Harvard University, working on what he came to define as paradigmatic changes in anthropological theory. In 1982 he published an important article titled "Anthropology, past, present, future: Toward an anthropology of anthropology"[14] and noted that anthropologists had created their discipline by studying origins and today were studying the present with an ethnological focus. But, he insisted, humans had always been interested in the future; an awareness of the future shaped and affected their lives. He therefore proposed, as others were beginning to do, that the future should

---

[12] At Harvard he recommended that his friends should read E.H. Carr's *What is History* (published in 1964). In an essay, published in 1976, he wrote that he offered the essay in the spirit of a remark by Carr: "the more sociological history becomes, and the more historical sociology becomes, the better for both".

[13] *The Human Direction: An Evolutionary Introduction to Social and Cultural Anthropology* (with James L. Peacock) (New York, Appleton-Century-Crofts, 1970), and now in its third and revised edition, was translated into Japanese in 1975 and has also been translated into Thai and awaits publication.

[14] "Anthropology, Past, Present, Future; Toward an Anthropology of Anthropology", in E.A. Hoebel, R. Currier, and S. Keiser (eds.), *Crisis in Anthropology: View from Spring Hill.* (New York and London, Garland Publishing Co., 1982), 91-108.

become a legitimate focus for a new generation of anthropologists.

An unexpected circumstance gave him the opportunity to reaffirm this concern. A series of annual lectures had been endowed by the Golay family in honour of Frank Golay, a distinguished economist and one of the earliest members of the Southeast Asia Program, and Tom played an enthusiastic role in launching the series. His correspondence in these years (1994-1998), occasionally in the form of the long memoranda he favoured, reveals him as urging vigorously that the implications of the dramatic pace of change in Southeast Asia should be a central topic in contemporary Southeast Asian studies[15] and therefore an appropriate focus for the "Golay Memorial Lectures".

Evidently, he had been thinking earnestly on these lines during the upsurge of energy in the final years of his life. He was well aware of remarkable changes overtaking Thai society and elsewhere "out there" and was also, of course, mindful of the direction that he had long urged anthropologists to take. In his opinion, changes in the region represented fundamental dimensions of life such as "space, time, proximity, distance, affections (e.g., love and hate), and health and well being, the essential quality of life for Southeast Asian peoples, past, present, and future". A year before he died, he summed up the urgency of the situation in no uncertain language:

> It strikes me as inescapable that the religious, political, economic, social organizational and familial orders in Southeast Asia (and the rest of the world) have already undergone transformations that might only a short time ago have been deemed too fantastic even to contemplate.

So convinced was he that priority should be given to these developments that he would not accept that other and more recent academic pursuits—which he dismissively referred to as the "post toasties"—should be allowed to steal a scholar's attention. In a somewhat heated letter written to an overseas friend in February, 1997, he insisted that one must not be diverted from "thinking about, addressing, or even perceiving (much less engaging) the pervasive disjunctions and transformations that affect the lives of the peoples of Southeast Asia, or anywhere else, or the social and cultural forms that are being transformed and changed". Furthermore, he realised to

---

[15] It was his suggestion that the Fifth Golay Lecture should be accompanied by a conference. At school he was top of his class in "civics", and it is tempting to believe that our undemonstrative colleague had been long ago endowed with a lively social conscience.

his grief that the global market was today the latest instance in world history of a large-scale transformation and that it was accompanied by moral disarray and frequent violence. What lay ahead of this globalising and deplorable situation was "the future" that needed to be studied, and to do so meant that one had also to take into account the past and present, "a trajectory" of historical experience. He was fond of the expression "trajectory".

In this way a new paradigm for regional studies could emerge, and "globalisation" was his obvious candidate. But, as he wrote to the same friend, it should be studied:

> for the future—not "today" but "tomorrow". And, unlike the preferred model of previous area studies [i.e., "traditional" polities], any new perspectives cannot privilege "us" as models of what tomorrow will be like but must incorporate "us" as both actors and acted upon along with all those "others".

The Golay Memorial Lectures probably gave Tom pleasure by providing him with an unexpected context for voicing ideas developed earlier in his life and also, perhaps, for racing against time when doing so, for he was perfectly aware of the gravity of his physical condition. But an event that took place not long before he died undoubtedly brought him contentment, and this was when friends of Harvard days, colleagues, and former and present students came together at Cornell from many centres in the United States and several disciplines. On 19-20 February, 1999, the anthropology department, with the cooperation of several other Cornell departments, centres, and programs, organised a two-day interdisciplinary symposium to celebrate his career.[16] The theme chosen was an appropriate one: "Religion, Society, and Popular Culture". Professor James L. Peacock, of the University of North Carolina in Chapel Hill, introduced the symposium with a moving address: "Applied Weber/Kirsch/Parsons". Eight papers were delivered, and the proceedings were notable for the deference accorded Tom and his career. A friend commented that "no big egos were involved on this occasion". The sincerity of the homage and the depth of affection displayed were striking. A reception was held in the Kahin Center, and guests declared their feelings for him. One speaker went so far as to attribute to him qualities associated with a Bodhisattva. Later that evening Tom was overheard to murmur: "I would have

---

[16] The Fall 1999 *SEAP Bulletin* contains an account of the symposium held in his honour.

liked to have known that guy".

The timing of the symposium was perfect. About a month later his condition began to deteriorate rapidly. He never recovered and was transferred to the Ithaca Hospicare Center, where he endured his suffering with characteristic tranquility. Never alone, he sometimes bewildered his visitors by speaking Thai. Students were at his bedside to the end. A Westerner in Thailand had asked one of Tom's former students why the Thudong monks (forest monks) of Thailand, about whom she had written, were prepared to undertake dangerous risks. This student, always with Tom in his final days, consulted him. Tom asked for his electrolarynx and taught for the last time.

> To understand why Thudong monks were not afraid of death, we need to examine their beliefs in karma, or rebirth in multiple lives. So strong was their faith that they believed that if they got killed, say by being attacked by a tiger or wild elephant, they still had another chance to be reborn and in their next life try to make progress toward enlightenment. In other words, if they do not succeed in this life, there is always a next life in which to try again.

> By contrast, Westerners generally do not believe in rebirth; they think that they have only one life to live. The typical Western Buddhist is determined to meditate his or her way to enlightenment in this life. As a product of the prevailing culture (belief in one life), they tend to be more cautious. You can't be reckless because you might blow your only chance to get enlightened.[17]

He died peacefully on 17 May.

This memoir is written by a friend and program colleague but not by an anthropologist. Others will be qualified to judge Tom's scholarly status, and it is hoped that they will acknowledge that he left behind a substantial body of writing in spite of heavy administrative duties and the tragedy that prevented him from completing what he intended to achieve: a study of the changes over the years that affected his two

---

[17] I am grateful to Dr. Kamala Tiyavanich for relaying and commenting on Tom's words. He was reiterating what he had long taught. See, for example, *American Anthropologist* 12, 2(1985), 304. Tom was no longer in a physical condition to explain that the monks were fearless (*kla*) in face of danger and death, not only because of their faith in the possibility of spiritual development over many lifetimes, but also in the protective power of the Dharma always conferred on those who themselves followed and protected the Dharma.

Thai families.[18] He also intended to write a commentary on his collected articles that would, as he put it, identify "what I think their
'trajectory' is".[19]

He was a reserved person, but observant and with steely resolve
and a sharp analytic focus. His was a complex personality. He was in-
clined to keep to himself and never sought the centre of the stage.
Sometimes he may have been unassuming to the point of self-efface-
ment. In his last years he confessed that he seemed to find himself to
be "cranky" and in the uncherished role of "naysayer". He was always
quiet even before 1992. A friend of many years has observed how Tom
would tend to "whisper" words of wisdom when commenting on current issues. He was, however, always ready to be consulted and would
answer enquiries with magisterial handwritten notes, accompanied by
references, comments, and sometimes regrets that a subject had so far
received insufficient attention. He gave the impression that he had
mastered a canon of invaluable literature to be shared whenever an
opportunity arose. He had a wry sense of humour, mischievous eyes,
and an impish smile. A friend has said of him that his smile was gentle,
"but I always felt that I needed to prepare myself for a droll remark
when I saw his smile". Tom was unquestionably considerate and is
gratefully remembered as a friend in time of need.

Some may have imagined that he was passive, but this does not
mean that he did not influence others. On the contrary, his influence, albeit subtle, was profound. One reason was that he invariably

---

[18] Yohko's reminiscences of his 1992 return to his village will be published in Professor
Jonsson's collection of Tom's work. He very much wanted to write about the situation of
religion in Thailand today. In a letter to his overseas friend, dated 14 August, 1996, he
noted: "If it has not already happened, it is on the way for Thai Buddhism to develop a
full-scale 'Reformation'....All too often 'religion' is seen as a 'constant', but it is always a
'variable', and this is especially the case in Thailand today. The ferment in Thai religion in
general and Buddhism in particular is changing many of the cultural parameters that have
been fundamental in Thai religiosity".

[19] Two pages of undated typescript, addressed to the writer of this memoir, were found
among Tom's papers. He had decided to make some biographical observations as well as
note "some of the thematic notions that run through the several essays the program might
consider bringing out". He added that "after all, this is not the greatest story ever told
and can, under any circumstances, always be changed". He may have foreseen that others
might have to edit the final version. Alas! The typescript got no further than his M.A. and
never explained why he chose Thailand. All he says, and rather mysteriously, is that, when
students ask him how he "happened to choose Southeast Asia as the region where I would
work, the answer is not so clear as how I got into anthropology as a discipline. The path to
both was not especially straight."

attended the annual meetings of the AAS [Association for Asian Studies] and the American Anthropological Association. He was a convention *aficionado* and knew every German restaurant on the convention circuit.[20] He therefore had ample opportunities for informal conversation with friends and colleagues, often his former students, and his comments on what they were doing would be sought, remembered, and treasured. His opinion was never lightly ignored.

Tom's summing up of the ground covered during a panel in honour of the late Lucien Hanks may give a glimpse of how it felt to have an informal conversation with him. One would soon gather that one was being "encouraged" or assured that one's work provided "food for thought" and might even be "ambitious", "intriguing", or providing "a provocative hypothesis, worthy of further consideration". Yet perhaps something more was at stake, and Tom would then begin to think aloud and wonder whether "it might be that...". At the same time one would be gently reminded of insight of other and earlier scholars. Eventually, one would be offered suggestions and maybe recommendations for considering additional aspects of one's study. But he would always be courteous and perhaps sometimes even playful, and he would certainly disclaim the right to make "assertions", even though one would probably end up with having to acknowledge that further research was still necessary. In the meantime, Tom's distinctive approach would have come across; the "social and cultural aspects" of whatever was being studied had to be taken into account. Moreover, if the subject impinged on Buddhism, one would be reminded that substantial research had indicated the "dynamic role of Buddhist values, ideas, and institutions" among Tai peoples. And so one would go away with the feeling of having received warm encouragement and useful hints for further lines of investigation from a learned but modest scholar.[21] A friend, who, still a young Thai student, first met Tom at an AAS meeting, recalls that "he never made me feel as if I was a struggling student, or that I were Thai for that matter. He treated me as a fellow traveller in quest of a better understanding about Thai society. He made me feel that I 'belonged' in that group of scholars".

---

[20] Memories of Tom need not suppress his appreciation of good food and his own culinary skills. He enjoyed disconcerting friends with a horrifying description of the sensation that accompanied the consumption of Japanese-style "dancing (drunken) shrimps".

[21] "The Quest for Tai in Tai Context: Forethoughts and Afterthought", *Crossroads* 2, (1990), 69-79.

Another and major reason for Tom's influence was that his students could readily spot a teacher who had much to offer and would take trouble with them. A colleague who shared courses with him remembers his delight in his students' creativity and how they would respond by outdoing themselves in meeting their own standards. Their tribute on the occasion of the symposium in his honour explains convincingly why they held him in esteem. In spite of his disability, he had won their attention and affection by sheer intellectual integrity, and they expressed their debt in personal terms. He had "opened our eyes", "pointed us forward". He respected "our ideas, our work, and our individual projects in a way that encouraged us and challenged our intellectual horizons". He "guided us to become our own anthropologists in order to sustain the discipline and keep it vital". They had no difficulty in recognising his qualities as a teacher: his encouragement of creative projects; his love for and skill in introducing them to their discipline's intellectual foundations, upon which their projects rested; encouragement to explore new areas of anthropology, even if they were "trendy". "You point, but you never push; you question, but you never cross out". Other and characteristic glimpses of him were recalled: how, for example, he would put notes and clippings into their boxes by way of carrying on an interrupted conversation, how he would have an eye on the future "when issues would be resolved one way or another, or all ways imaginable—and some unimaginable", and his fondness for quips. He would explain that the candy on the seminar table was evidence that "God is in the details" or would counsel that "in the great garden of anthropology we should let a hundred flowers bloom. However, we should probably recognise that there is a difference between flowers and weeds".[22]

Tom may not have visited Thailand very frequently, and yet his *rapport* with Thai was remarkable. It was as if he did not have to go to their country to become close to them. One former Thai student has even suggested that one could forget that he was not Thai. Here, then, is the final source of his enduring influence. He has sometimes been described as a revered teacher, and this he was to his Thai students in a special way. He exemplified what for them was the powerful and enduring teacher (*ajan*) and student (*luk sit*) relationship. He had *jai yen* ("a cool heart"): he possessed equanimity and could meet

---

[22] I am grateful to Tom's students for sharing their fine tribute with me.

all situations. They could see him as a selfless and compassionate being who practised the ethical standards of a Buddhist. He was a good
and kind man who taught by personal example just as the Buddhist
teachers he had known in his village did. He listened to those who
approached him and always had something helpful to say. According
to one Thai friend, he had the reputation of having *aroma dee* (a "good
disposition"), he was *jai dee* ("kind"), his was "the heart of a monk"
(*jai phra*), and he had *yim suai lae yim samer* ("a beautiful smile and
was always smiling"). The same friend visited Tom in the hospice and
observed how he exuded good will, kindness, and enviable serenity.
"It was close to visiting one's favourite monk at a temple. It was good
therapy".

The Thai poet, Sujit Wongthes,[23] receiving the news that Tom
had just died, immediately wrote:

> Ajan [the teacher] Kirsch was born and died in
> the West
> Then he willed his spirit to [the Province of]
> Mukdahan,
> Where on the banks of the Mekong the human
> world links to the world below.
> His spirit has now made its way to the highest
> heaven in the skies.[24]

When he was in the hospice, Tom had asked that his friends in
the village where he studied long ago should be told that he was dying

---

[23] The poet's wife, Pranee Wongthes, was among the first group of Tom's students, and
his daughter Tom's last Thai student. Professor Pranee organised a symposium at Chiang
Mai University to express the gratitude of Thai anthropologists for Tom's contribution
in encouraging the discipline of anthropology in their country. The symposium, titled,
"Friends in the Field: Four Decades of Anthropological and Sociological Studies in
Thailand", was held on 28 January, 2000, and about fifty scholars were present to honour
Tom.

[24] The poet is invoking the Theravada teaching of the three levels of existence, well-known
in Tom's village in the Isan, or northeastern Thailand. According to Lao belief there, the
world beneath the earthly plane is where the powerful Phya Naga lives. The Isan has special
access to that world, and the poet is conveying an Isan impression of Tom and seeks to
lay him to rest in his beloved northeastern Thailand. "The highest heaven in the skies" is
reserved for those who have only done good deeds. I am grateful to Dr. Kamala Tiyavanich
for bringing the poem to my attention and for discussing it with me, and I am also grateful
to Dr. Craig Reynolds and two of his Thai friends for a translation that gives effect to the
Isan animist belief that the river links the three different levels of existence. The poem
appears in "Ajan Kirsch of Cornell: A death that left us speechless", *Sinlapa Watthanatham*
[Art and Culture], 20, 9 (July 1999), 130-131.

and that he had requested his ashes to be taken to the village Wat. The poet knew this.

Yohko honoured Tom's wish. His ashes were deposited in a *chedi* erected inside the Wat Traiphun compound, a privilege usually reserved for deceased monks.

Selected List of Major Works
by A. Thomas Kirsch

Books, Monographs, and Edited Symposia

Human Direction: An Evolutionary Introduction to Social and Cultural Anthropology (co-authored with James L. Peacock). New York: Appleton-Century-Crofts. 1970. (Second Revised Edition, Englewood Cliffs, New Jersey: Prentice-Hall. 1973; Third Revised and Expanded Edition, Englewood Cliffs, New Jersey: Prentice-Hall, 1980.) Translated by Koichi Mizuno as *Shakai Hatten to Kindaika: Shakai Bunka Jinruigakuteki Sekkin* 社会発展と近代化：社会文化人類学的接近 (Social Development and Modernization: A Social-Cultural Anthropological Approach). Kyoto and Tokyo: Minerva Press. 1975.

*Feasting and Social Oscillation: A Working Paper on Religion and Society in Upland Southeast Asia. Cornell Southeast Asia Program Data Paper No. 92. Ithaca, New York. 1973.

Changes and Persistence in Thai Culture: Essays in Honor of Lauriston Sharp (co-edited with G. William Skinner). Ithaca, New York: Cornell University Press. 1975.

Symposium: Religion and Society in Thailand, (Organizer and Editor). *Journal of Asian Studies* 36(2): 239-326. 1977. (Available as a separate reprint from the Journal.)

"Phu Thai Religious Syncretism: A Case Study of Thai Religion and Society." Ph.D. diss., Harvard University, 1967.

Articles

*"Nong Sung: A Changing Phu Thai Commune Center in Northeast Thailand." originally written for C. Cunningham ed. *Villages in Thailand* that did not materialize. 1968.

"Development and Mobility among the Phu Thai of Northeast Thailand," *Asian Survey* 6(7): 370-378. 1966. (Reprinted in R.O. Tilman, ed., *Man, State and Society in Contemporary Southeast Asia.* New York: Praeger. pp. 481-489. 1969).

"Loose Structure: Theory or Description?" in Hans-Dieter Evers, ed., *Loosely Structured Social System: Thailand in Comparative Perspective.* Yale University Southeast Asia Studies, Cultural Report Series #17. New Haven. pp. 39-60. 1969.

"The Thai Buddhist Quest for Merit," in John McAlister, ed., *Southeast Asia: The Politics of National Integration.* New York: Random House. pp. 188-201. 1971. (abridged version)

"Economy, Polity and Religion in Thailand," in G. William Skinner and A. Thomas Kirsch, eds., *Change and Persistence in Thai Culture: Essays in Honor of Lauriston Sharp.* Ithaca, New York: Cornell University Press. pp. 172-196. 1975.

"Modernizing Implications of 19th Century Reforms in Thai Sangha," *Contributions to Asian Studies* 8: 8-23. 1975. (Reprinted in Bardwell L. Smith, ed., *Religion and Legitimation of Power in Thailand, Laos, and Burma.* Chambersburg, Pennsylvania: ANIMA Books. pp. 52-65. 1978.

"The Evolution of Thai Values," in Lauriston Sharp, ed., *Thailand Since King Chulalongkorn*, Asia: Supplement #2, Spring 1976. pp. 67-83.

*"Kinship, Genealogical Claims and Societal Integration in Ancient Khmer Society: An Interpretation." in C.D. Cowan and O.W. Wolters, eds., *Southeast Asian History and Historiography: Essays Presented to D.G.E. Hall.* Ithaca, New York: Cornell University Press. pp. 190-202. 1976

"Introduction: Symposium on Religion and Society in Thailand," *Journal of Asian Studies* 36(2): 239-240. 1977.

"Complexity in the Thai Religious System: An Interpretation," *Journal of Asian Studies* 36(2): 241-266. 1977.

*"The Thai Buddhist Quest for Merit," in *Clues to Thai Culture*, compiled by Central Thai Language Committee (OFM). Bangkok: Kanok Bannasan Press. pp. 120-136. 1981. (expanded version of 1972 article)

"Notes on Thai Religion" in *Clues to Thai Culture*, compiled by Central Thai Language Committee (OFM). Bangkok: Kanok Bannasan Press. pp. 146-163. 1981.

"Buddhism, Sex Roles and the Thai Economy" in P. Van Esterik, ed., *Women of Southeast Asia.* Occasional Paper #9, Monograph Series, Center for Southeast Asian Studies, Northern Illinois University, Dekalb, Illinois, pp. 16-41. 1982.

"Anthropology, Past, Present, Future: Toward an Anthropology of Anthropology." in E.A. Hoebel, R. Currier and S. Keiser, eds., *Crisis in Anthropology: View from Spring Hill.* New York and London: Garland Publishing Co. pp. 91-108. 1982.

*"Cosmology and Ecology as Factors in Interpreting Early Thai Social Organization." *Journal of Southeast Asian Studies* 15(2): 253-265. 1984.

"Text and Context: Buddhist Sex Roles/Cultures of Gender Revisited." *American Ethnologist* 12(2): 302-320. 1985.

"*Khwamsabson Nai Rabab Sadsana Khong Thai.*" (Thai translation of "Complexity in the Thai Religious System" 1978) Journal of Thai Studies, Institute of Thai Studies, Thammasat University, August 1985, pp. 7-48. (special number on Religion in Thai Society)

"The Quest for Tai in Tai Context: Forethoughts and Afterthoughts." *Crossroads* 5(2): 69-79. 1990.

*"Cosmological Factors in the 'Collapse' of the Khmer and the 'Rise' of the Thai: Speculations." in John Marston, ed., *Anthropology and Community in Cambodia: Reflections on the Work of May Ebihara*. Melbourne: Monach Asia Institute. forthcoming. The Spanish version in John Marston, ed., *Antropología y comunidad en Camboya y Tailandia: Reflexiones sobre la obra de May Ebihara*. Mexico City: El Colegio de México. forthcoming.

* Selected for an aborted book project to publish Tom Kirsch's collection of works (see Tsuji p. 65 in this volume).

www.ingramcontent.com/pod-product-compliance
Lightning Source LLC
Chambersburg PA
CBHW072140280526
45788CB00002B/720